Fear and Joy

A life in and out of nappies

By

Ben Ingram

Title: Fear and Joy - A life in and out of nappies

Author: Ben Ingram
(ben.ingram71@gmail.com)

Editor: Michael Bent

Publisher AB Discovery

© 2018

Images copyright © 2018, Vincent Russo.

You can find more at

https://bigfordiapers.deviantart.com/

www.abdiscovery.com.au

Other Books from AB Discovery

Sissy Babies – The Ultimate Submissive

The Joy of Bedwetting

Overlapping Stains

The Babies and Bedwetters of Baker St

The Bedwetter's Travel Guide

The Joy of Nappies

Growing up a Bedwetter

Three Sissy Babies

Six Misfits

Six Misfits – A man and his dog

The Six Misfits – the seventh misfit

The Adult Baby Identity – coming out as ABDL

The Adult Baby Identity – Healing Childhood Wounds

Living with Chrissie – my life as an Adult Baby

The Adult Baby Identity – a self-help guide

The Adult Baby Identity – the dissociation spectrum

Becoming Me – The Journey of Self-acceptance

Living happily as an Adult Baby

Adult Babies and Diaper Lovers – a guidebook

There's still a baby in my bed!

So, Your teenager is wearing diapers!

Where Big Babies Live

Home Detention

Adult Babies: Psychology and Practices

Coffee with Rosie

Being an Adult Baby

The Three Chambers

A Brother for Samantha

Mummy's Diary

The Hypnotist

Chosen

The Snoop

The Washing Line

My Baby Callum

A Baby for Felicity

The Regression of Baby Noah

A Baby for Melissa and her Mother

Baby Solutions

Discharged into Infancy

The English Baby

A Mother's Love

The Psychiatrist and her Patient

The Reluctant Baby

The Book Club Baby

The Rehab Regression

The Daycare Regression

A Woman's Guide to Babying Her Partner

The ABC of Baby Women

Me, Myself, Christine

Diaper Discipline and Dominance

The Epitome of Love

Australian Baby: a life of nappies, bottles and struggles

Fear and Joy: a life in and out of nappies

The Fulltime, Permanent Adult Infant

Contents

INTRODUCTION

F or the past forty years, I have had to keep a secret.

It's in my existence every day. There is no escape from it and no cure for it. Unless you have a similar desire, pleasure or urge to do something harmless, but which modern society would frown upon, you will never fully understand.

Some people might say, as would I, *"What is normal and acceptable?"*

Most have only been exposed to people like me who have non-conforming desires, likes or pleasures such as wearing a nappy through exaggerated representations in the media. What they don't understand is that it isn't simply a habit we can stop or break. In the mainstream narrative, people that wear nappies - either for comfort or desire - are usually described as freaks, weirdo's or worse. For myself and other people like me, this behaviour comes with deep shame and stigma, as we are told by society that it's unusual, unacceptable and not normal.

Fear and Joy – a life in and out of nappies

Personally, from an early age I knew I was odd for wanting to wear nappies, and in a time before the internet and social media, I was very much isolated and alone with my feelings. Coming to terms with it has taken me on journeys of both laughter and heartache. I am fully aware through items I have read or watched on TV that if anyone found out, I would be ridiculed by most, as this is not an acceptable form of normal behaviour in society. Wearing a nappy is not a disorder for me. It doesn't impede my everyday activities and in fact, I am just like most 'normal' ordinary people, working ordinary jobs and leading a somewhat ordinary life. I don't look different on the outside. Unfortunately, it is human nature to associate these 'peculiar' lifestyles with more sinister roots. This, however, is so far from the truth! Our society's narrow-mindedness for people who are 'different' means we reward conformity and normalcy and ridicule different lifestyles that we don't or won't understand.

In the past, attempts to fight this desire have often resulted in buying nappies and then throwing them away out of extreme guilt. This binge-purge cycle is apparently regarded as a symptom among those who haven't fully come to terms with what they do, and the shame and guilt attached to it. In an ideal world, I wouldn't need to hide who I am, and I wouldn't need to fear or worry about what society would say. When it comes to something (or someone) that is different from the world we're used to, we fear and mock, sometimes with violence what we don't understand.

This book, 'Fear and Joy, A life in and out of nappies' is a true account of the early parts of my life up until age twenty-four. To protect both my family and friends in this book, I have changed their names. I have no doubt that quite a few people can relate to what I experienced and how it moulded me to become who I am today. It has taken a long time for me to come to terms with some aspects of my childhood following the help of a trained counsellor in recent times, who has written a few words below. I now embrace the past and have learned to accept who I am today.

Fear and Joy – a life in and out of nappies

It took a long time for me to decide whether or not to put my memories into a book, as I was recalling some memories I would rather have forgotten. I must admit that while writing, I did also recall good times and memories that made me feel happy. There are a couple of people in the book that I would love to meet again. These are the people that helped me at a particular time or event that was happening in my life and gave me hope that nice people actually do exist. I do believe that these people entered my life for a reason. What they did for me were things I had not expected at the time. Looking back though, I'm just so glad they were there and were able to both lift my spirit and confirm that human kindness and acceptance for who or what you are is sometimes all it takes to bring a smile.

Do I blame anyone for what happened? Not at all. As an adult now, I do believe the punishments were a bit harsh and not necessary. Maybe if the internet had been around and my parents could have researched this, the outcome may have been different. With the exception of some teasing by my brothers and stares from people while out in public, even the parts that I thought were awful at the time, I don't think were really so. After all, I was just a kid wearing a nappy, most people wouldn't have even noticed me, let alone commented on what I was wearing. Would you?

I hope you enjoy reading this book. It has certainly been a good help to me, recalling my thoughts and memories from that time of my life as in some way it helps me to understand more of who I am now. If you did enjoy it, please let me know at *ben.ingram71@gmail.com*. I would welcome any feedback or comments about what you have read, both good and bad. This is my first time writing a book and I have other memories as I got older that one day I might write down.

Personally, I enjoy reading true accounts and stories as opposed to fictional stories. It helps if I can associate with the character in the story or account being told and I hope I have been able to do this for you in this book.

Thank you for taking the time to read my story and if you had similar experiences I hope it has helped you to know that you were not the only one.

After reading my book my close friend who is a professional Psychologist wrote this for me to include in the book:

Ben and I met many years ago when he had just started a relationship with my Auntie. At this point in time, he was still finding it hard to accept himself and so he was introduced to me on a professional level to see if I, as a counsellor, could help him through that.

We started working through his feelings by email at first as Ben still found it very difficult to talk about these things face to face, but once we had made some progress he felt comfortable having face to face sessions. Our sessions, combined with the support of a good partner, helped Ben to understand himself better and really make good progress in accepting himself as a person.

Ben and I no longer need to see each other on a professional basis but we remain good friends and it has been an honour to be involved in this project. Since our sessions ended, he has taken huge steps forward himself and, despite finding some areas of the book difficult to write, he has turned his bad experiences into a positive in order to try to help others that may still be struggling to accept themselves. I am extremely proud.

Jemma Harrison, Psychologist

Chapter 1 - Aged 6

Well, it's 1977 and summer was finally here.

It seemed to take forever to come that year. I remember we had finished school on Thursday at dinner time and my brothers and I were now looking forward to a whole six weeks off. This normally meant lots of playing outside with my brothers and friends who lived in the street, staying at my grandparents' house more often, visiting my dad and basically not having a care in the world. Mind you, this also meant more trouble for my mum, as we did get into some scrapes. I must admit, I hated school from the start and I wasn't a great pupil, even at a young age. I just wanted to play and have fun, and this was the case throughout my entire school years.

I remember it was 1977 because it was the Queen's Silver Jubilee and there was bunting up in nearly every street we walked down. Spanning from house to house, bright coloured Union Jacks were everywhere, and all the local shops were selling souvenirs of the occasion. Numerous street parties were being held to commemorate this major occasion and the one I attended was amazing. I loved it.

These parties were what living in a small community was all about. Everyone mucked in and had a really good time. All the kids sat at long tables in the middle of the road, drinking squash and eating like there was no tomorrow. My brothers and I always got carried away at these type of social gatherings, getting over-excited and most of the time ended up getting shouted at by either my mum or whoever was her boyfriend at the time, or our local babysitter. I was nothing serious, just the normal "how many times have I told you?" and "if I have to tell you again" complaints. I dreaded hearing anyone shout that at us at the time, but now I find myself using the same types of phrases - only modernised - on numerous occasions.

A typical 1977 Jubilee street party.

My dad left not long after my younger brother was born, so I don't really have any recollections of him being around. We would visit him on weekends as he was back living with my Gran and Granddad around the corner. Mum was a single parent with a boyfriend now and again, so she relied on getting help from family members that lived in the area and family friends who lived nearby. Money was very tight at this time, so having three kids to look after meant we didn't have much. Treats were few and far between. Holidays never happened, but we got by and we were a happy little family. I can't imagine that that being a single mum with three kids our age was a great turn on for any prospective boyfriend. Some were okay, some were non-descript.

The one of note and who is mentioned in this account turned out to be another total arse. His name was Robert, he drove a brown Chevette and lived nearby, and to be honest looking back now I don't think he liked us but tolerated us, so he could be with my mum.

I was six years old now, my older brother was seven and my younger brother was five. We lived in Manchester in a two-up, two-down terraced council house in not a bad area. It was a nice street and everyone knew each other, helped each other out and knew everyone's gossip, but the one thing about everyone in this street is that they all looked out for each other. This is something that I miss these days. I know some people who don't even know their next-door neighbours.

Our house was basic with no indoor toilet, but we did have an outside lavatory. Yes, an outside lavatory and our back yard led into the back alley where we could play safely with all the other kids on the street. We got into some major scrapes and bother playing in the alleys. However, at least when you got caught by a parent or grown-up, they would give you a quick whack and that was it. You stopped doing what had gotten you into trouble and respected the adults. The whole street knew each other, as there were lots of young kids that all went to the same school or nursery, so it was like a mother's meeting place in our house and on our street daily!

My Grans outside toilet. Very cold in winter!

So, where do I start with my memory of this time in my life?

I was six years old and I was still put into nappies for bed. My mum had tried so many times to get me out of them, but with a wet bed most mornings decided that putting me back into night nappies was the best option. I think the constant hassle of taking my bedding to the laundrette every other day proved too much in the end. I'd wet the bed and we didn't have a washing machine at the time. All the other normal washing went to my Grans each week, as they had a modern top loader!

Don't get me wrong. I didn't wet the bed every night, but sometimes it would have been two or three nights in a row, then dry for two or three more. I must admit I hated waking up in a wet bed and dreaded my mum coming in and finding out, not because she would shout at me or anything, but the look of despair at yet another laundry trip was clear on her face. The first time I was put back into nappies at night, I didn't really think much of it, to be honest, only the fact that my younger brother didn't have to wear one for bed, but I did. It was also marginally better than waking up in a wet bed.

If I was ever staying over at anybody's house prior to being put back into nappies for bed, I would always be made to put a nappy on "just in case". Sometimes they were dry in the morning, sometimes not, but wherever I was, nothing was ever said by the family member or friend about a six-year-old still wearing nappies. It was what it was and the routine of getting ready for bed was always the same and I just accepted it, as I thought this is what other parents or kids had to do with this problem. I had been dry during the day since I was four, but I did struggle with the whole toileting concept, so I was still wearing nappies full time in the daytime well when I started nursery. Consequently, I had to go home at dinner time or my mum would have to come in to change my nappy every day. Again, I didn't think anything of it. It was just the normal routine for me and no one said anything, or if they did, I never heard it and so, I just got on with life quite happily! I suppose my mum was lucky that the nursery was only around the corner from where we all lived.

A typical 1970's laundrette where my nappies were washed.

At six years old, I was still having the odd day accident, but thankfully, as these were not often, it was pretty much overlooked. This was during the same period that my mum decided to put me back into nappies for bed on a semi-permanent basis to ease the washing burden. As it was 1977, a nappy consisted of the good old-fashioned white terry towelling cloth squares, two pins and a pair of plastic waterproof pants. Not the comfiest of nappies when wet I must say, but not too bad when a nice dry clean one has just been put on. Disposable nappies were available as I now know, but no one I ever saw had one on as they were very expensive and terry towelling was the traditional and cheapest way to nappy your kids. This was to change very soon, but having never seen one, I didn't even know they existed.

When I used to go around seeing a member of the family or if we popped around to the next-door neighbour's houses, every garden I went into had a washing line up constantly during the good weather. Several pairs of plastic pants and at least half a dozen nappies would be blowing in the wind getting dry and funnily enough, most of the time, they were mine. Another obligatory item in these households was a white nappy bucket, either in the bathroom or in the kitchen. My mum must have gotten tired of our bucket, as I was still using it at six years old and there were always at least two used nappies in there soaking away ready to go to the laundrette to be washed properly - or my Grans if we were visiting that day.

A usual sight in most gardens - particularly mine - for years.

Thursday night was pretty much a normal routine kind of evening I suppose. The only exception was that this night we were very excited. The next day we were going for a long weekend to Blackpool, our first real holiday as kids. As normal, we had tea watching the TV, which was only three channels then, so pretty much you watched whatever was on. There was never any arguing about who wanted to watch what, not like nowadays. As normal, around 6:30ish most nights, we would all get ready for bed, pyjamas on and so forth. We were then allowed till about quarter past seven when my younger brother and I had to go to bed. My older brother was allowed a little longer. This crucial time was the interval for 'Emmerdale' and the only available slot for mum to get us ready before 'Corry' came on - an absolutely 'must watch' programme for years for my mum. At the allotted time of 6:30, mum came down as usual with the pyjamas and we all got undressed. My brothers dressed themselves into their PJs and I put my PJ top on then sat on the carpet watching TV waiting for my mum to put my nappy on, a ritual which I had gotten well-used to by now.

Mum came in from the kitchen with the essential terry nappy and plastic pants and said "Right, buggerlugs. Lie back."

Back I went still trying to watch TV, then with one swift movement, my bum was lifted off the deck the nappy slid underneath me, pulled up between my legs and fastened securely into place with either two blue or white-tipped locking nappy pins. My mum would then scrunch up the leg openings on the plastic pants on one side to allow one foot to go through it, then the other, then with one swift movement, positioned them ready to go over my nappy. She lifted one leg and pulled up one side of my plastic pants, then the other leg and the job was done. I then stood up and mum helped me put my pyjama bottoms on, as these were bought for me when I had stopped wearing nappies at night so were not really big enough to accommodate a nappy. They were not that tight, but not loose either and unless you were blind, it was easy to notice that I was wearing a nappy underneath the bottoms. As for how it felt, well, when you're a baby and wearing nappies you don't know any other feeling until you're taken out of nappies and get big people underwear. So, imagine wearing big boy underwear all day and then having them taken off you and a bulky nappy put in its place. What does it feel like at that age you may ask? Well, the only way you could possibly imagine it is if you go to your bathroom, grab a bath towel and pin it on yourself like a nappy then tape a black bin liner over the top. Then you get the feeling I had as a six-year-old after my mum had expertly sorted me for the night.

Once we were all done we were allowed about 3/4 hour playing. It was a really nice evening, so we were allowed to play in the back yard as well, which pleased my mum, as she could have some peace and quiet in the house while she watched a bit of TV.

As always, she would yell out, "Don't get dirty and keep the noise down!"

As we played in the back, I could hear lots of other kids playing too. Summer was great and with the added excitement of our impending trip the next day, we were all really happy and having a great time playing in the yard. It's good to point out here that this was the evening that I started to realise and became conscious of the fact that at six years of age, I still wore nappies to bed - something that had never happened to me before.

Up until now I just put one on as normal and even when mum told me I was going back to wearing one for bed, I just accepted it as I had the many previous occasions it had happened. Coupled with the following few days - also being the first time I was made to wear the nappies in the day time again (although not as a punishment, but as a safety option for my mum) - I started to become very self-conscious and at times embarrassed about the fact I was now six years old and back in nappies again day and night.

About seven pm that evening, I heard a knock at the door. As soon as mum had opened the door I could tell straight away it was Janet from two doors down. She was coming to Blackpool with us along with her seven-year-old daughter, Louise and two-year-old son, Josh. We had been friends with them for as long as I can remember, each mum looking after each other's kids when needed, babysitting, favours - the normal things neighbours did in those days. It turned out that Janet had brought the kids around as well, as she needed to borrow a suitcase since hers had broken earlier that day while packing. Not having a spare suitcase, my mum decided to visit my Grans house which was about a fifteen minutes' walk away, as they would have one. We didn't have a phone in our house, so walking there was the only option. My mum told us she was going to Grans for a while and Janet would look after us and we could stay up later till she got back. I asked if I could go with her as I loved seeing my Gran and Granddad, but she said no as I had got my pyjamas on ready for bed.

"Go and play in the yard love, I won't be long," she said.

Brilliant news! More playing out time.

We all went into the back yard, which included Louise, as she was my older brother's age, so they knew each other well from school. Josh stayed inside with his mum, as it was past his bedtime anyway. We had a good laugh playing and mucking about. We remembered that mum had told us to be careful and not get dirty, but as normal, while we were playing jump the paddling pool - which is a great game as the loser gets soaked - I had not quite made it.

It was pretty obvious to anyone that this would happen, given the fact that I was trying to run, jump and stretch while wearing a nappy with pyjamas that were a bit on the tight side. It didn't quite work out. I landed on the side of the paddling pool with one foot and I fell backwards and landed on my bum in the water that was left from the previous day. Good news for me though in one sense, as I was wearing the nappy. It broke my fall and whereas normally your bum would hurt for ages banging on the concrete underneath the pool, it didn't hurt as much, but my pyjamas were soaked.

We all giggled and laughed like mad. I did too, as it had happened so many times before and is just as funny when you have seen it for the twentieth time, as when you saw it the first time. It's that look of instant shock as you hit the cold water. It didn't take long for Janet to come out and ask what we were all laughing at, before she spotted me, standing in the middle of the pool with water dripping off me. She burst out laughing too.

Quick as a flash while still laughing, she shouted, "Get inside! If your mum comes home and finds you like this, she'll go mad, love!"

As I walked towards the house, it now became apparent to me that the water had literally soaked the nappy my mum had just put on me earlier. It was sagging quite a bit and made me walk noticeably different. It didn't dull the laughter, even from me. As I got into the living room, Janet had a towel and beckoned me over.

"You silly boy," she said. "Your mum will have a fit if she came back now. Where are your pyjamas kept?"

"Upstairs," I said. "Under the bed".

With that, she went upstairs and came down with a dry set of pyjamas. "Take your pyjamas off sweetheart and put these on before your mum comes back and finds out".

As I dropped my pyjama trousers, I couldn't help but think, "My nappy is soaked and I can't hide it."

As Janet turned towards me to help me put my top on, she glanced down and for a split second stopped.

"Oh! You're still in nappies love. I had forgotten. I thought it was only when you were away from home now. Are you still wetting the bed?"

"Yes," I replied. "But only for bedtime though."

I felt a bit embarrassed, as this was the first time someone had questioned the fact I still needed a nappy for bed.

"It's okay, love. Don't worry. Are the nappies still in the cupboard upstairs?"

Janet had babysat many times, so she had a good idea where everything was.

"Yes," I said in a bit of a saddened voice.

"Don't worry sweetheart. I can sort you out and get you changed before your mum gets home. I'll go and get a dry one and get you changed, okay?"

She returned with a new nappy and plastic pants and just like my mum, she told me to lie on the floor. She took off my plastic pants and then unpinned the absolutely soaked nappy and with a smile she said, "At least it's not this wet in the morning. You'd need swimming lessons if it was!"

Just like mum did, she pinned the cloth nappy on and very expertly lifted each leg to get the plastic pants up and over to cover all the towelling. She ran her fingers around the leg openings of the plastic pants to make sure that all the cloth was inside the elastic and then finally gave a quick final pull up on the waistband when I heard a voice at the back door. It was Louise.

"Mum?" She said, but with a pant and puff, as she had still been playing outside for the last half hour, "what time are we going home?"

"As soon as Diane gets back, love," she answered.

"Okay," she said and then in all innocence, she asked "Why have you put Ben in a nappy? Isn't he too old for a nappy now?"

"He still has accidents love. You did until you were four, if you remember."

"Yeah, but I didn't have to wear a nappy!"

"Well no, but it's not a big deal, is it? Go outside and play or I'll put you in one!" she laughed.

With that, she turned and went back to play in the yard with my brothers.

"Shame Josh isn't awake Ben. I could have done his nappy at the same time!" she said. Josh had been asleep for the last half hour on the settee and still needed to get his pyjamas on.

Once I had stood up, Janet then helped to put my pyjamas back on. As I expected, she struggled to get my pyjama bottoms over my nappy, but they went up in the end and with that, she very gently patted my bum a couple of times and said "There you go, sweetie. All done. I'll tell your mum it was my fault, I spilt water over you okay? I don't want you getting into trouble. Big day tomorrow, isn't it?"

"Yes," I replied quite excitedly. "I can't wait!"

"I bet you can't," she said. "Well, go and carry on playing now, Ben. Your mum should be home soon."

With that, I waddled back outside, the pyjamas bottoms being a little bit tighter than the others, clearly indicating to anyone that saw me that I had a nappy on. I mentioned earlier about starting to become conscious that I still wore nappies. Hearing Louise say what she did and Janet being a little shocked when she first saw me standing there with a nappy on was possibly the start of it. Not that I blame her in any way at all, but it's the first time I had realised that at my age, wearing a nappy was maybe wrong or something. I was kind of hesitant to go outside, but I went towards the back to carry on playing none the less, thinking that well, she didn't laugh at me, and Janet was really kind about it, so it'll be okay.

As I continued to wander outside I heard my mum return and it was a perfect way to get out of going outside and I returned into the house to say hello to mum.

"What have you been up to?" she asked. "It's okay Diane. It was my fault. I took the kids a drink out just after you left and I slipped and bumped into Ben, who was standing near the paddling pool." She was laughing as she said it.

My mum laughed and then looked at me and asked, "Did your nappy get wet love, or is it okay?"

I could see Janet looking at me and again she interrupted.

"It was soaked Di, but I found a dry one upstairs and changed it."

"Ah, thanks, Janet. He's been back in them for about two months now. Too many wet beds, weren't there, Ben?" She gave me a kind of woeful look.

"It's okay," said Jane. "Louise was the same for a bit. He will grow out of it when he's ready."

"Bloody hope so!" my mum said, "I've changed enough nappies to last a lifetime. I thought I'd be done with washing nappies by now!"

"Right Di, I'll get Louise and I'll shoot off. I'll be back tomorrow morning at about nine. Come on Louise, we're going!"

And with that, Louise came running in and gave me a kind of weird knowing look - or what I thought was one anyway. Janet bent down to give me a kiss and hug and while doing so, winked at me, confirming her original intention that she was saving me from the earlier incident I had found myself in and all was well.

Janet grabbed my bum and gave it a squeeze and a pat saying, "See you tomorrow, squishy bum!"

The rest of the night continued as normal and about 8:30 we were all in bed, looking forward to the trip tomorrow. It was going to be great. Our first proper little holiday. The weather had been good for the last few days and I was so looking forward to seeing the beach, the sea and the famous tower which my granddad had been telling us all about for the last week.

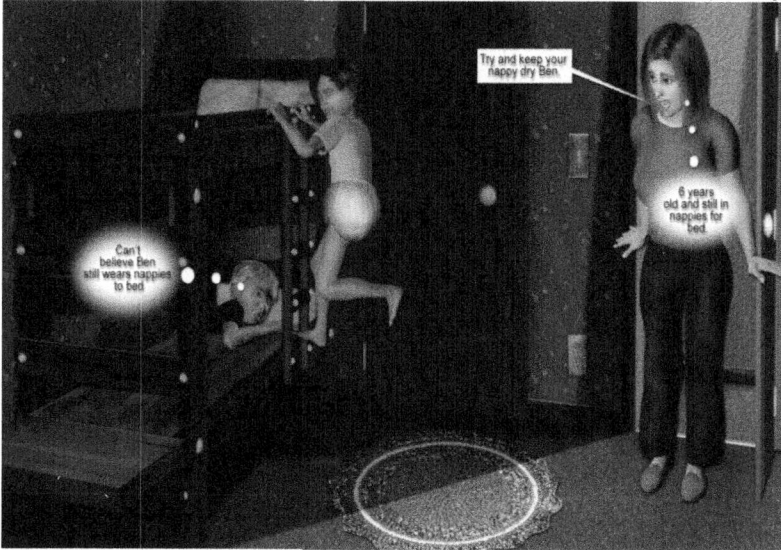

This is what my mum probably thought, having to put a six-year-old into nappies every night.

The following morning, we woke up about 8ish. The big day was here, and my brothers and I were up and about in no time. As on every other day, we all went downstairs and into the parlour. This was the room at the front of the house where all our toys were and where we were told to go and play if my mum had guests or family were around and kids were to be out of sight. It was also a similar morning for me as there was no dry nappy this morning, which meant sitting around in a wet nappy until mum got up. I would then be put back into big-boy underwear, but as I needed to be washed first, I had to wait for mum to do it for me.

Wet nappies in the morning were always a bit uncomfortable and as I got older, were getting even more so, as I was more active and wanting to do stuff a child in a nappy wouldn't normally do. In the winter or cold months, wet nappies were even uncomfortable as they made you feel cold, which only added to the misery of either sitting or playing with a wet towel wrapped around your body with plastic pants holding the sagging nappy in place. It wasn't long before we heard mum coming down the stairs.

"Morning kids!" she exclaimed.

"Morning mum!" we all replied together, not looking up from what we were doing.

"Come here Ben," was her next routine sentence.

I got up and walked over to my mum standing in the doorway. She was always dressed in her pink dressing gown and flowery slippers. She leant over me and pulled my pyjama pant waist and plastic pants away from my waist, so she could have a feel of my nappy.

"Wet again," came the inevitable reply. "Come on, love..."

And with this, we wandered into the kitchen. I stripped off to my nappy while mum filled the sink with warm water. She would then pull down my plastic pants, unpin the nappy and then lift me up in the sink while she washed me.

"I really hope you're going to stop this soon, Ben," she exclaimed with exasperation. "You're six years old now and should be able to keep your bed dry. Alex is five and he doesn't wear nappies anymore, does he? "

Alex was my younger brother and had grasped the toilet concept really quickly, as had my older brother Steve. It was just me who was still struggling.

"Remember the rule, love," she repeated. "Three dry nappies in a row and you can stop wearing them at night again and see how we go."

I sighed and said I was sorry, to which my mum replied, "It's okay Ben. It's not your fault, but we are going to have to sort this out soon if you keep on needing nappies."

I was also still having the odd accident in the day, which really displeased my mum, but they were getting better gradually. Once I was cleaned and dried, I was lifted back onto the floor and told to put my pyjamas back on. I then went back to play with my brothers while mum had a cup of tea. Looking back now, I was very fortunate in that she did this first when she came down. If it was nowadays, I would have to have at least one brew first, so I am very grateful for that. As I made my way back to the parlour for some reason, I remembered the previous night and the look Louise had given me and the slight shock of Janet.

Was I really too old to be in nappies and what would other people think if they saw me now?

That night was the start of when I began to feel self-conscious about wearing nappies. All the people on the trip would now know that I wore nappies to bed and might make fun of me or something.

As I entered the parlour my brothers yelled, "Come on Ben, grab a car it's race time!"

And with that, we were soon enjoying playing and once again, I again forgot about my questioning thoughts.

So, who was coming on the trip to Blackpool? Well me obviously! My two brothers, mum, and her new boyfriend Robert. (I'll explain a bit more about him later. Suffice to say, we hated him), There was also Janet and her two kids. Also coming along was Jane, who was about fourteen or fifteen years old and our regular baby sitter. She was great and such a laugh. My mum's sister, Auntie Karen and her daughter Sharon made up the final two members of the holiday party. Sharon was three and to add more to my mum's despair - and sometimes mine - she was fully toilet trained in the day by age two.

She still needed a nappy at night, but as my auntie would frequently point out if we were on a sleepover or she was at our house, "Isn't Sharon doing well now! Two dry night nappies this week. We will soon get her out of night nappies!" Sharon always cheered this, and it only made me feel even worse at times.

Another kid that's beaten me to being nappy free!

Fear and Joy – a life in and out of nappies ▌

As soon as breakfast was finished, mum told us to go upstairs, get dressed and to pack a couple of toys in each in our school bags. She had laid out all our clothes and was hoping to leave mid-morning. She also reminded us that Robert would be arriving soon and we were to be on our best behaviour. I found out later that he had funded the whole trip for us all.

Robert was about thirty years old. He'd been with my mum for about four months or so at the time of our holiday. I suppose like all boyfriends or girlfriends of a parent, they always seem okay at first. Then again, I suppose just like us, they are on their best behaviour with their respective partners to make a good impression. At first, he was okay but soon got to be someone that we hated. He had his own way of dealing with us if we had done wrong and I must admit that at first, I liked him more than any of the other boyfriends my mum had had. It didn't take me long though just to tolerate him and keep out of his way. Not surprisingly, I was the one he disciplined, shouted at or pushed around the most. This stemmed from a trip to the zoo a month earlier where unfortunately for him, I had a wee accident in his car.

Was it my fault? I don't think so.

We had been out all day and, on the trip back home we had fallen asleep in the car. We had drunk lots of squash and water during the day and as I was really tired, I must have fallen into a deep sleep pretty quickly. When I was woken upon arrival at home, I knew instantly I had wet myself. Robert went nuts. He had only had the car a short time. It was his pride and joy, and I had messed up the back seat. My mum tried to calm him down, which worked thankfully and said she would clean it up and it would be like new again. With that, we went into the house straight upstairs where we were told to get into bed. As normal, I waited for mum to come up to put my nappy on which she did fairly quickly.

As I lay on my bed and while she did the normal routine, she said, "Of all the things to do today Ben, why? I know you didn't mean it, but why didn't you tell me you needed the toilet before we left the zoo? This has got to stop Ben do you hear me, it's not fair on Robert or me is it?"

"No," I said, and with that, she pulled up my pyjama bottoms and went to bed.

The morning of the trip, Robert turned up and went into the kitchen with my mum while we continued to play in the parlour, so excited for the journey ahead of us. Janet soon arrived with Louise and Josh, followed shortly by my Auntie Karen and her daughter, Sharon. There was only Jane left to come now, but she was always on time so we all had fun playing games and messing about while the adults chatted and drank cups of tea in the kitchen and living room.

This was what Roberts Chevette looked like.

We were having so much fun and were all really excited about going away that day. After a short while, just as Jane arrived, my mum came into the parlour and told me to come with her. As I left the room, I saw Jane and said hello and gave her a hug and proceeded to follow mum upstairs. I was a little bit nervous, as I thought I might be in trouble or something and as kids do, I started to wrack my brain, but nothing of noteworthy of a telling off came to mind, so it lessened the fear a bit.

As I followed her into her bedroom, she shut the door behind me and said, "Ben, I know you won't like this, but I'm putting you in a nappy today for the trip to Blackpool."

"Why?" I sighed, "I won't wet myself I promise! I don't want to wear a nappy, everyone will laugh at me."

Since the episode the night before, I had become a little more conscious and aware of the fact I wore them and for the first time, someone had questioned it, and now I was going to be out in a nappy in the *daytime.*

"You've never bothered before, love," came the reply.

"I know, but I don't want to wear one, mum," I sobbed.

I had started to cry, as I had horrible thoughts of others now seeing me.

"Well, we don't have a choice, Ben. Robert was furious when you wet his car the other week and I can't take enough clothes if you do have any accidents. I also want Robert to be in a good mood, don't you? No one will notice, and it's only just in case, sweetheart".

It was no good arguing, so I just said "Okay," in a sobbing voice.

With that, she lifted me on the bed, removed my shorts and underpants and slid an already prepared terry-towelling nappy underneath me and expertly pinned it in place. Next came the obligatory plastic pants and the job was done. As she pulled up my shorts, it became apparent that they would not go over my nappy and cover it properly, which made me hope she might change her mind as surely, I could not go out with these shorts on?

Wrong.

My mum went off into my bedroom and came back with a slightly bigger pair that my older brother had grown out of a while back. She lifted me off the bed and onto the floor and told me to step into the shorts, gently pulling them up over my nappy and fastening them in place with a belt. As they do, terry nappies and plastic pants tend to bunch up and puff up when getting covered. My nappy was clearly visible above my waistline, so my mum did her best to tuck it all in and kept pulling up the shorts until it was completely covered.

Mum then pulled down my t-shirt and said, "There you go love. All done. Go back downstairs and play in the parlour until we need to go. No one will know you've got it on, okay?"

Mum getting me ready for the Blackpool trip. That nappy

felt huge under my shorts!

I started to walk down the stairs, and this is the first time that I really felt anxious and conscious about my nappy. It felt very bulky under my shorts and it made walking just that little bit more difficult than normal. For the past few months, I'd not worn a nappy in the daytime, as I was doing so well - apart from the zoo incident - even on trips out. The only time was bed-time and I didn't care about that.

I looked down and there was a definite bulge there and from my perspective, anyone looking at me would instantly notice that I had something on under my shorts. I walked to the parlour as quickly as possible, so that hopefully no one would notice. I am just thankful that my mum probably knew that I couldn't fully conceal a nappy and so had given me a longer than a normal T-shirt to put on which, while walking, covered my bum enough. Any other activity, however, would have made my t-shirt rise up a bit at the back and this was inevitable. So, I assumed some of the nappy would be showing at times. Goodness knows, it took my mum a bit of time to tuck it all inside my shorts. It was plain to anyone looking that I was wearing a nappy... in the daytime. I was six years old and this terrified me.

As I entered the parlour, Steve beckoned me over and announced, "You're on my team, Ben."

They were playing 'armies', so I went over sat in the floor and carried on, quickly forgetting the last fifteen minutes and the fact that I had the biggest nappy on known to man! Well, that's what it felt like every time I moved!

"Come on kids! Time to go!" yelled Mum. "Grab your travel bags."

We all screamed excitedly and hurried towards the front door. It must have looked like the end of a football match just as the turnstiles opened, as we all spilled out onto the streets. My brothers, mum and I headed towards Robert's car, while the rest of us got into Janet's car. Six in one car! Well, it was the 70's, so Sharon being only three sat on her mum's knee in the front! Try getting away with that now!

As I climbed into the car, Robert looked at me and said with a scowl, "You better not wet the seat again young man otherwise you will be in trouble."

"I won't", I said in a calm voice and a cheeky smile, confident that I wouldn't, as I had a nappy on.

He started the engine and we were off.

As we drove down the street my mum turned to look at us in the back, "Boys, are you looking forward to seeing Blackpool tower and the beach?"

"Yeeeah..." we all screamed together. "We're going to have a fabulous time, aren't we!"

Just before she turned back, she glanced at me, winked and whispered, "Are you okay, Ben?"

"Yes mum," I replied.

"Good boy," she said and turned to the front and chatted with Robert.

As soon as she said that, some of the fear and anxiety I had at being put into a nappy eased a little. I realised that mum was okay about it. She's just asked me if I'm okay, so I can relax a bit and enjoy the journey. As I'd been wearing the nappy for about an hour now, it had moulded itself to my body a little, so that while of the bulkiness had gone, I could still tell I had one on. Thankfully, the car moving along and taking us to Blackpool took my mind off it and my thoughts were on the next couple of hours and the journey ahead, where we were going for three nights in a bed and breakfast guest house.

It wasn't long into the journey and all was going well. We were progressing slowly through the countless streams of cars on the roads of other families making their way to their holidays. The car was hot, the windows were down, and my mum was doing her best to entertain us. Watching the scenery as we drove fascinated me. I'd never really been out of Manchester until now and when we hit the first motorway, it was like a race track to me. Wow, the speed of the cars and the endless miles of road in front of us were amazing. We had only just picked up speed when it all clogged up again, a bit like it still does today. Slowly but surely, we made our way north towards

Blackpool, passing the same car a few times as drivers were switching lanes to try and get ahead a little.

After about two hours and only a few miles gained, Robert had had enough and wanted to stop for a break. The car was getting hot and we were getting restless, so the next service station was the next stop for us. As we pulled in, I was amazed at how these places were run. It looked huge. We had never been to a motorway service station before and it was another adventure en route to our holiday. We parked, and Janet pulled alongside us. We were all excited and shouting at each other through the open windows.

"Quiet, quiet!", mum shouted. "Right… everyone out and wait on the pavement."

We all got out and talked excitedly to each other and then like the animals entering Noah's ark, we all marched up to the main building. The place was just packed with people. It was a toilet stop first and we were split into three parties. My brothers went with Robert while Louise, Josh, Jane and Janet went to the ladies while mum, Sharon, my Auntie and I went to the family room. It turned out Sharon was also wearing a nappy for the trip, due to the time it could take, but she hadn't used it and was asking for the toilet. I suppose it made sense that I went with them. The queue was really long, and I kept asking mum how long it would take as I needed to go.

"Not long, love. Just hold on."

Minutes passed, but it seemed like hours to me. My auntie had soon had enough and didn't want Sharon to have an accident, as she was doing so well out of nappies, so she decided to go to the disabled toilets, so she could have a wee. Mum and I kept waiting patiently, while she asked me if I was having a nice time, to which I agreed with a childish high pitched, 'Yes'.

The queue was moving very slowly, and I whispered to mum, "I needed a wee really bad."

"I know love, but I can't push in."

Everyone else was finished by now, including Robert who was gesturing to my mum to come with him. At this point, she took my hand and led me towards the shops and the rest of our party. I was really busting to go now, and I started to cry a bit when mum bent down beside me.

"Ben love, your gonna have to wee in your nappy," she whispered. "I don't think we are going to get in a toilet for me to take your nappy off."

"I can go in the grid outside, mum," I replied quickly.

"I'm not taking your nappy off outside, Ben. Just have a wee, otherwise, everyone will be waiting, and you won't have time to get a drink and some sweets. It's okay. I won't shout at you".

I was quite upset at having to wee in my nappy, as I'd never done it on purpose before. I can honestly admit it was a weird and strange trying to do it. It was as if my body was saying 'no' and my brain was saying 'have a wee' at the same time. I was led towards the sweet counter so I could choose my sweets and as I stood there deciding what to have, I finally let go. As I started to wee, once I started I couldn't stop, and I could feel my nappy getting wetter and wetter. It was really warm, not at all like the cold wet nappies I woke up to most mornings. As I stopped weeing, I picked up a chocolate bar and handed it to my mum. I headed to the tills with her and as I walked my bum felt horrible, huge and my nappy felt really, really wet. Within a couple of minutes, the nappy had done its job and absorbed all the wee and as usual, the good old plastic pants had stopped any leaks.

By the time we had paid and were heading back to the car, I had gotten used to the feeling and like before, it had moulded itself once again to my body and I continued as normal. As we got back to the car, Robert asked if everyone was sorted and that we were to get back in the cars, so we could carry on to Blackpool. As I went to the door to open it my mum took my hand and led me to the back of the car. She leant over me pulling the back of the waist of my shorts away from my bum, putting her hand inside my nappy pants to see how wet my nappy was. This was something I was certainly used to! Normally, if I wore one 'just in case' it was usually still dry, and I'd be happy, but this time I knew it would be wet. However, I had no idea how wet it would be after my first deliberate wet nappy.

"It's okay, Ben," she said. "It's not that wet. I'll sort you out when we get there, okay?" She gave me a little smile and a hug and said, "Let's go, and don't worry Ben, it's not your fault."

Our journey to Blackpool continued and we were so excited and amazed by the traffic and speed of all the cars. It wasn't long before we were playing *'first to spot the tower'*, all scrambling about the back seat trying to get the best view, looking for this famous big tower. By now, I had completely forgotten about the nappy I was wearing and was enjoying the trip again. If I'm being honest, it wasn't that uncomfortable as I had gotten used to it - as if having a nappy on was normal for me. We were soon nearing Blackpool when we finally spotted the tower. Wow, it looked amazing and very big and this made us even more excited.

"Nearly there, boys," my mum said.

We were still gesturing to my Auntie and the others in the car behind, waving frantically back and forth at each other and smiling. After leaving the motorway, we travelled down a long road and eventually turned onto the promenade not far from where the 'pleasure beach' was located. Wow, we were all stunned at how amazing the place was. There were hundreds and hundreds of people walking about, clambering to get onto the beach and to get to whatever activity they had planned. It was amazing, and I was immediately in awe of this place. As we made our way up the promenade, I realised I needed a wee.

In one split second, I thought to myself, "I'm wet already so I may as well just wee in my nappy again, as mum had said it wasn't that wet and that it was okay to do it!"

So, as I continued looking out of the window, I decided just to let go. I only did a little wee this time, but the same feeling came over me as the nappy started to absorb this little toileting incident.

I thought to myself, "This is okay! I don't need to worry. No one knows I've wet myself and Robert won't get mad as I would have wet his seats if mum hadn't found me a toilet in time."

In addition, having already been told to use my nappy, I wouldn't get in trouble. So, with these thoughts in my head, I just carried on enjoying the journey to where our guesthouse was located without a care in the world.

We soon arrived at our lodgings for the weekend and were greeted by a lovely lady who welcomed us to Blackpool. She said that she would look after us for our short stay and ensure we had everything we need to make our holiday a time to remember. We had all escaped the cars and were in the reception area signing in and getting our room keys when Jane (our babysitter) came over to me and said that I had a wet patch on my bum and had I sat in anything. My Auntie Karen who knew I had a nappy on, overheard Jane and immediately sussed that my nappy must have leaked. I'm not at all surprised really, knowing what I know now. I had just wet myself whenever I needed to go for the last two hours, and as I had emptied my bladder at the service station as well, I think I had gone past the capacity of a cloth nappy. I couldn't be blamed really. I had never known how much a nappy could hold, so I had probably weed in it too much.

Auntie Karen just said, "It's ok, dear. When we get our rooms, we will sort you out."

I just smiled thinly and turned to my mum who just whispered "It's okay love. Don't worry".

Once upstairs in this lovely guest house, we were split up into rooms. My mum, Robert and my youngest brother in one room. Janet, Louise, Josh and my older brother were in another room as he was the same age as Louise. In the final room were my Auntie Karen, Sharon and Jane in another room with me. Mum probably thought that if she was to keep Robert in a good mood, it was best to put me in a different room, as I was still wearing nappies at night, something that Robert didn't agree with and often, even though he had only been with my mum a short time would make that feeling known to me.

Sharon still wore nappies to bed, so we could be looked after in the evening together by either my mum or Auntie as Janet had Josh to look after. Jane had accompanied us to Blackpool as a family friend, but also to help look after us kids, which she loved doing. My mum had asked her to help look after me and my three brothers, so she could spend some time with Robert.

As we got into our room, there was a huge double bed which is where my Auntie Karen and Sharon would sleep, a single bed for Jane and a small camp bed in the corner for me. Compared to our house, these rooms were massive. I also spotted an indoor toilet yes, a toilet in the room. There was also a small area to make tea and coffee. We were all having a look around the room when the guesthouse owner, Mrs Williams came in with a small grey bucket and placed it into the bathroom. She explained to my Auntie that if she puts all the used nappies in there, she will ensure they are washed, to give the parents a break.

"That's really kind of you," replied my auntie "We have three in nappies. Are you sure you're okay with that?"

"Oh yes," she replied. She looked at my cousin Sharon, who was now just walking around the room with just a nappy on. Sharon was about to have hers removed, as she didn't need a nappy until bedtime. She asked where the other two who wore nappies were to which Auntie Karen replied, "Josh is next door and also Ben here."

"I'll get another bucket then for next door and leave it with them," the lady replied.

She didn't even raise an eyebrow that I was still wearing nappies. I suppose she has seen many children being put into nappies when on holiday so as to not ruin the bedding if they are still having accidents. So again, I thought this was okay then, I don't have to worry.

A nappy bucket was a common sight in our house for a long

time!

"Here you go, Ben," Mum said, as she came into our room with my items of clothing that she had unpacked from the case. "Sort these out and put them in the drawers. Jane will help you."

Jane gladly replied, "Of course I'll help you. Come on, Ben."

As she took the stack of items off my mum, on top were about six nappies, pins and about four pairs of plastic pants in various shades of white, as they were all well used by now and should have probably been thrown away.

Jane turned to Karen and asked where she had put Sharon's night nappies to which she replied, "I've just left them on the side to air. Just leave them at the end of his bed, we all know where they are then for when he needs to put one on."

As I turned towards my bed, my mum noticed my wet patch, which I had forgotten about.

"Ben, come here a minute," she said.

As I turned towards her, I suddenly remembered that I had made my nappy leak. She felt my bum and then as normal, felt inside the nappy and said in an exasperated tone, "Bloody hell, Ben. I only told you to use it at the shops, have you been using it all day?"

I slowly replied "Yes…"

"Well your shorts are dirty now, aren't they? They will have to be washed," she continued. "Come on… We will have to ask Mrs Williams to wash them for you."

And with that, she told me to take off my shoes so that she could remove my shorts. I stood there in now in just my t-shirt and a very wet nappy and after agreeing to a time to meet up for going out, she took my hand and led me downstairs to where Mrs Williams was in the dining area. I can remember walking down the stairs praying I didn't meet anyone, which thankfully I didn't.

"Ask the nice lady, Ben," my mum said. "Please, can you wash my shorts for me."

"Of course, I can," she replied.

"He's wet them," mum said, "I'm so sorry."

"Ah it's okay," she replied. "These things happen. I'll have them ready for later this evening."

As we walked back up the stairs mum said to me that I had to learn to take a bit of responsibility and that was the reason she took me downstairs to ask the question myself.

"I didn't tell you to keep using it, Ben, did I?"

As we neared the landing Robert was coming out of his room and looked at me with a disgusted look as I walked past him.

"What's happened this time?" he spat out in a stern voice.

"His nappy leaked. Nothing serious," replied my mum.

"Oh, for goodness sake, it's about time you grew up! Six years old and still wetting yourself! Are you not ashamed, lad?"

I just nodded and looked down at the floor. My mum told me to wait outside my room while she had a word with Janet in her bedroom about meeting up in the front lounge in about 1/2 hour. She then went into my room to speak to my Auntie.

As mum came back out, she looked at me and said "Ben, I can't deal with this type of stuff this weekend. We are all here on holiday to have a nice time and I don't want any more accidents. Is that clear?"

"Yes, mum," I replied.

"Right, go and see Jane and she will clean you up while I sort your brother out."

I went off into the room where Sharon was now obviously nappy free and ready to go out. Jane called me over and told me to lie on the bed. Jane was a nice girl from what I can remember. Very softly spoken, she did well at school too and loved looking after my brothers and me. She sometimes had a boyfriend when she was babysitting, but she always made us happy and did her best to look after us. I lay back on the bed and Jane slid Sharon's changing mat under me. She had done my nappies a few times when babysitting so I didn't mind nor was I embarrassed.

"Blimey, Ben" she laughed as she pulled off my plastic pants. "This nappy is soaked. I'm not surprised your mum was a bit mad!"

She then unpinned my towelling nappy, folded it up and placed it in the bin that Mrs Williams had provided. My Auntie then came in with a small bowl, flannel and some soap. Jane did the obligatory wipe down and dry to make sure I didn't get a nappy rash. Once I was dried, she lifted me off the mat and went to the clothes pile to get some underpants. Result: no nappy… But in a little sort of way, I was a bit unhappy I think. I had found that using my nappy when I wanted to, allowed me to not have a care and I could forget about having accidents. Anyway, undies on, clean pair of shorts and I was ready to go out.

We all met in the entrance hall and we set off for our first adventure in Blackpool. As we exited the guest house, the smells were amazing. Candy floss, doughnuts, burgers and just an endless sea of souvenir shops and eateries. It was amazing, the first time we had ever seen anything like it. We could hear and smell the sea and couldn't wait for our first time on the beach. We soon stopped at a small café, as we hadn't eaten since the snack stop earlier that day. We all had chips out of a cone and a drink then set off again towards the beach. As we approached the beach, we could smell the donkeys, something that I miss these days when visiting Blackpool and the sea air was also something I had never experienced before.

As we walked down a kind of jetty slip on to the sand, I'd completely forgotten that I was now nappy free. Having been wearing a nappy most of the day and just going when I wanted to, I just forgot, and at that moment, I let go. No sooner had I let go, I felt wee running down my legs. Real instant panic set in. There was no way I could get away with this one.

"How is this my fault?" I thought to myself. "I've been in a nappy most of the day, so how am I to blame?"

It was too late, however, as Louise who was a few steps behind me had noticed and did not hold back telling her mum that I was weeing. My mum turned around, as did Robert and asked me if I had. I couldn't lie and said it was an accident and that I forgot I didn't have a nappy on.

"Sorry, mum. I'm sorry," I spluttered.

Thankfully Jane stepped in, and said, "It's okay Di, I'll sort him out. You carry on to the beach and I'll go and get some clean pants for him."

"Thanks, Jane. You're an angel". As I turned around to walk back with Jane, I heard my mum add, "Probably best to put him back in a nappy for the rest of today. Maybe it was my fault. Can't keep doing this though. Are you okay to take him back to the guest house?"

"Yeah sure," Jane said, "I'll sort it out."

We turned around and with Jane now holding my hand, we headed off on the short walk back to the guesthouse. On arrival Mrs Williams was there in the hallway.

"Hello, you're back already?" she enquired.

"Yeah," Jane replied. "Ben's had a little accident."

"Oh dear, poor love," she offered sympathetically.

"If I give you these shorts, can you wash them with the others, as he's only got one pair of shorts left?"

"Yeah, of course. Just bring them down and I'll sort them for you."

"Thanks, his mum has asked me to put him back in a nappy for the rest of the day, so we shouldn't have any more accidents."

"Oh dear, never mind. It's a bit warm for the lad to wear a nappy."

We turned around and went up to our room. Jane put the changing mat on the bed like before and told me to take off my shorts and undies jump up on the bed. As I laid down, Mrs Williams came in holding something.

"Why don't you try one of these?" she asked. "Some guests often leave things behind and I save some stuff in case people forget."

"What is it?" asked Jane.

"It's a nappy," she said. "One of the new disposable ones, much better for parents when they are on holiday. It was left by a family with a disabled boy last week. You also don't need any plastic pants, and when they are wet you can throw them away."

"Great," said Jane. "We will try one, hey Ben?"

"I'll get you another to take out with you if you like. I think there is another one left downstairs."

"That would be great," Jane said.

My immediate thought was 'what on earth is this' that I was going to wear. I'd never heard of a disposable nappy before, let alone seen one. It had always been terry towelling and plastic pants.

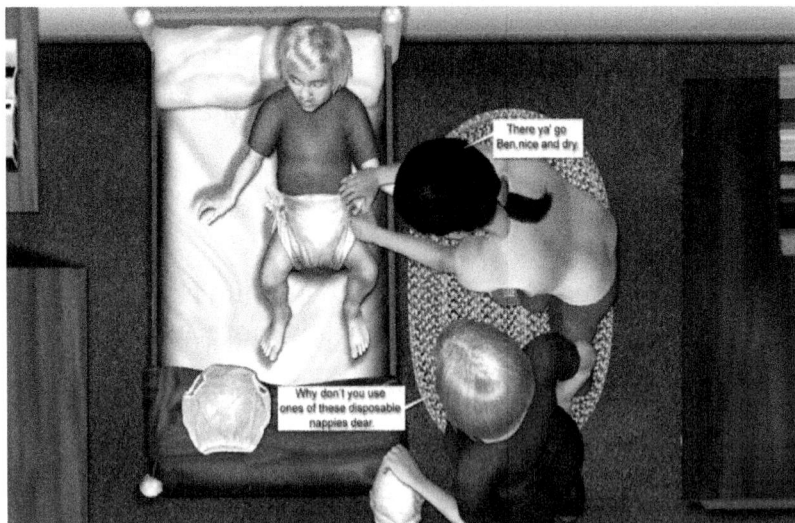

Jane was given a new disposable nappy to put on me!

As I laid there, Jane opened the white disposable nappy. It made a real loud crinkle type of noise and looked huge. She grabbed my legs as she normally did and slid the nappy underneath me. As my bum rested on the padding, it felt different from the cloth nappy I was used too. Jane brought up the front between my legs and positioned it as best she could.

"I hope this fits okay, Ben. I've never done one of these before."

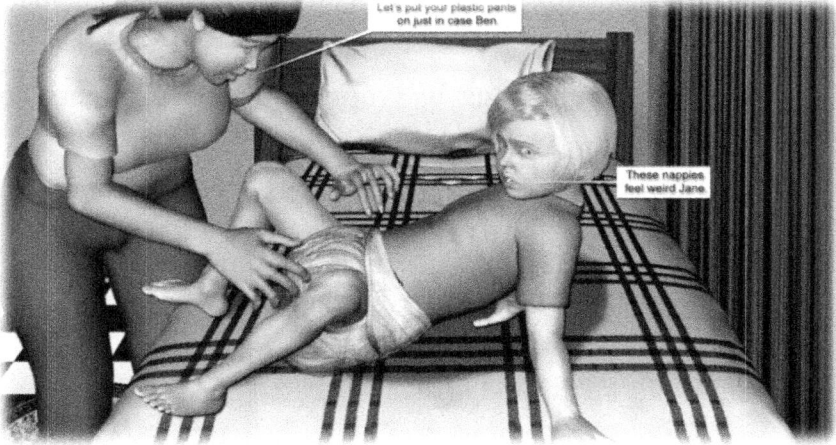

Let's put your plastic pants on just in case Ben.

These nappies feel weird Jane.

My first disposable nappy. It felt strange at first, but I liked

them better than cloth nappies in the end.

Jane had always put me and my younger brother in cloth nappies and was very good at it. She fastened up the tapes and then picked me up and stood me on the floor. My goodness! If I could go back to that moment now, I would! The disposable nappy was very thick between my legs, but at the same time felt comfier than a terry nappy.

"Is that okay, Ben?" she said.

"I don't like it! People will see!" I complained.

"It's okay, we will put your shorts on and it will be fine."

She fastened the shorts and hastened me out of the door to catch up with the rest of the family on the beach. As I walked towards the beach with Jane holding my hand, I remember being able to feel the nappy more than I could when I had a terry nappy on, even with the plastic pants. It felt like my bum waddled, and with every step, I could hear the slight crinkling of it, something a terry nappy never did. Little did I know then that this type of nappy was made of paper and plastic-backed. Jane then asked me if I was okay, to which I answered "yes".

Jane then told me, "Just use your nappy, Ben if you need to. I've got another one that the nice lady gave me in my bag."

She had been given the spare one from Mrs Williams. That meant only one thing to me, I was staying in nappies for the rest of the day and I was going to have to use it. At that moment I thought, fine, I've done it before earlier and now I've been told to again.

We met up with the rest of the family and once my mum saw us, she came over to me and Jane and asked if all was ok.

"Yeah," Jane replied. "No problem at all. Mrs Williams gave me one of those disposable nappies to use on Ben, so I put him in one of them if that's okay?"

"Yeah that's fine Jane," my mum replied.

"You okay, Ben?" Mum asked quietly.

"Yeah, I guess," I answered in a sullen kind of voice. Hearing my reply, she came over and knelt down beside me.

"Look, Ben, I know you can't help it, but we are all here to have fun. It doesn't matter that you've got a nappy on. No one will be bothered and as long as you have fun, that's all that matters isn't it?"

"Yes, I suppose so," I replied.

"Well, there you go then love, just use your nappy if you need to and we can go back to normal when we get home."

"But everyone will laugh at me, mum."

"They won't love, or they will be put in nappies too! It's easier for us all, Ben, as well as for you. You won't have any accidents, and no one will get mad and shout, will they?"

"Alright," I replied, still very unsure about this new development. "Jane said you have a real new nappy on, is it okay?"

"It's okay," I said, even though I was quite unsure.

"Good boy! Jane said they are for big boys like you. Now don't worry yourself and go and play with your brothers. If you need the toilet for a poo, just let me know and I will take you, okay?"

My brothers, Louise, Sharon and Josh were building sandcastles and I quickly joined in and was having a really really good time and I soon forgot the fact I was wearing nappies again! As the afternoon wore on, I soon had the urge to need the toilet. Well, I thought, I've got a nappy on and I wanted to see what happened if I wet this disposable nappy I had on, as I was curious about them. Just as I had been able to wet my nappy earlier in the day, I just sat there on the sand and let myself wee.

What a difference!

I didn't feel the wetness and it was just as comfortable as when Jane had put me in it earlier back at the guest house.

"Wow, these things are fabulous," I thought.

So, throughout the afternoon I just wet myself whenever I needed and what a relief it was! Josh was playing in the sand with no clothes on except his cloth nappy, which made me feel better as I had a big boy nappy on. Sharon was in her swimsuit and the rest of the kids in shorts and t-shirts.

Louise, however, sussed pretty quickly that I'd been put back into nappies and asked me quite blatantly. "Why have you got a nappy on Ben, aren't you too old now?"

"My mum makes me wear them," I replied, "It's not my fault."

"You're like a baby," she said, "Only babies wear nappies in the day like Josh." She continued in a teasing tone. "Ben's a baby! He wets his pants!"

"Louise, stop that!" Jane shouted at her and said if she carried on, she would be in big trouble. Jane soon came over and asked if I was okay,

"Yeah," I lied. "I'm okay."

She asked if I'd used my nappy yet and if it was okay.

"Only a bit," I replied.

"If you need the toilet, just let me know, won't you. If you can hold it and we can find a toilet, I will take you, so you don't have to use your nappy, okay?"

Jane was great, and I really like her for just being kind to me.

A couple of hours passed, and I was having a great time as were we all. Playing on the beach was absolutely amazing. It was nearing tea time and my mum and Auntie beckoned us all to come back and get ready to go back to the guest house for tea. We were soon all packed up and heading back while taking in the last moments of playing in the sand. Jane came over, held my hand and asked if I was okay.

"Yes," I said quite truthfully. "I've had a fun day".

"That's good," she responded.

As we got back to the guest house, Janet said she would go and sort Josh out then meet in the dining room where tea was being served. As she went upstairs with Josh, mum asked Jane to check if I needed a change, as I'd also been in my nappy a while now. Thankfully, she took me into the living room area and pulled my shorts down.

"It's a bit wet, Ben. Shall we put a dry one on?"

"Yeah I think so, it's not nice anymore," I replied.

Jane led me upstairs went and into our bedroom and just like before, she put the changing mat on the bed and lifted me onto it. She quickly removed the wet nappy and after a quick clean-up, she decided to save the disposable ones for the day and so put me back into a terry nappy. She did it very well and they always felt as good as when my mum did them. She talked to me the whole time, asking if I'd had a nice day too.

Soon I was wearing a nice clean nappy and I felt a lot comfier and with that, we went back downstairs and had a delicious tea, followed by lots and lots of ice cream, while we all chatted and laughed about the day we had just had. It was great.

And I wore a nappy all the time.

Blackpool in the '70s.

It was now early evening and, since we were on holiday, we did not have to go to bed at a normal time. The weather outside was still gorgeous sunshine, so it was decided by the grown-ups that we would go for a walk. Of course, I was in my nappy and the tighter-fitting shorts which Jane had put on, but as I had wet my other two pairs I had no choice. The idea of a walk didn't fill me with delight, but I wasn't bothered by it either. So, out we all went for a nice walk along the promenade.

As we crossed the road onto the beachside, mum said we could play on the beach, but not to get too dirty. Jane came down with us as did my Auntie, Sharon and Louise while Josh stayed with his mum, as he was in his pushchair asleep. Mum was walking hand in hand with Robert, keeping an eye on us as we walked towards the pier up ahead. There was a funfair on it and we were told if we were good we could go on some rides. As we got onto the beach, I was finding it difficult to keep up with my brothers when we were running, as wearing a nappy and shorts that were too small made running just a bit more difficult, but I did my best. Although a little bit upset with the fact I had to wear nappies in the day, I soon realised even at this age, that it was probably best as I did not want to incur the wrath of any adult if I wet myself, particularly Robert. As we neared the pier we found some steps and headed back up onto the path. Having run most of the way, only stopping to pick up shells and pebbles as you do on a beach, it wasn't long until someone noticed that my nappy was showing at the back as I climbed the steps.

As Louise passed me she said, "Wee, wee, nappy bum. You still wear nappies like a baby and I can see it!"

Louise was normally a nice girl. I don't think she really meant any harm by it - just a bit of kid banter as you do at that age. We got on well most of the time at home and played well together, and I suppose if it was the other way around I'd probably be doing the same and teasing her, so I just ignored her. As I got to the top, my mum came over to me and adjusted my shorts as best she could so that my nappy was hidden as best she could. I was wearing a t-shirt that covered half my bum, so at least I had a bit of cover!

We arrived at the funfair on the pier and we all were so excited. The noises of the machines and games being played were just amazing. Like before, I soon forgot the fact I had a nappy on and just joined in having fun with the rest of the kids and grown-ups. We were given 50p each to go and get some change. 50p coins in those days were huge and it was a lot of money to us. I went up to the cashier person and although not tall enough to see over the counter, I handed her my money and got some change in a small pot. I immediately went over to the 2p push slot games, like the ones on Drop Zone on TV. Mind you, it was hard choosing, as there were so many games all lit up and making noises.

The adults soon beckoned us over, as we were going on one of the swing rides outside. It was only for the kids, but it looked really fast and a bit frightening. It was the ride where you sit in, get a chain put across the front of the seating area and then you go around and around while it flings you out a little as you go faster. I'd never been on anything like this before, so I was both excited and scared at the same time. The ride stopped, and we were told to go and find a seat. The chairs were a little high, so my younger brother and I needed help up. Louise and my older brother were fine. Josh and Sharon were too young. As I turned around at the front of the seat, mum picked me up and placed me in the wooden seat. Surprisingly, as I had a nappy on, it was quite comfortable, even though it was wood.

The assistant came around and fastened the chains and the ride started. The ride was fantastic, and it felt so good having the breeze blow on your face and hearing all the other kids laughing and screaming. Soon it was over, and the ride came to a stop, the chains were undone, and we were told which way to go out. We were all very excited, laughing and shouting. As we got to where the adults were, we could see them smiling too and they were asking us if it was fun.

For me, the big news was that the nappy had made the ride more comfortable!

Next stop was the cafe area. It was about 7:30 pm and the place was still very busy. Of course, this was a wee stop for the kids and any adult who needed it. Jane came over to me and asked if I'd wet my nappy.

"No," I said, "But I need a wee."

"Okay, sweetie. Hang on."

She then put her drink down and led me to the disabled toilet, which was bigger than the rest. As we got in, it smelt awful - like someone had weed all over the floor a thousand times.

"Oh, my goodness!" Jane squirmed. "Ben, I can't take your nappy off in here. I think it is best if you just use your nappy like before and I'll let your mum know I told you to."

As I'd done this earlier in the day I just accepted it straight away and told Jane I would as long I didn't get into trouble with Mum or Robert.

"It'll be fine, Ben, I'll sort it," she said.

My shorts were a bit tight and I was hoping that being able to use the loo, Jane would have sorted my nappy out, as it had become a little uncomfortable and out of place when I had been playing on the way here. I told Jane my plastic pants were rubbing a bit and were hurting my legs. No sooner had I'd said it than she eased my shorts off to my knees because the floor was so dirty and adjusted my nappy and plastic pants, so they were in place again. I then had a wee in my nappy as instructed.

As we returned to the rest of the family, I was happy that I hadn't wet myself accidentally and had only weed as Jane had told me too. So, for me, it was a wet nappy again, but I knew it would be alright. In a wrong kind of way, I hoped they'd leave me in them, as I hadn't got into trouble for wetting myself and I could enjoy my day.

As I grabbed my ice cream, my mum came over to me and said that it's okay, Jane had told her what had happened.

"It's okay, Ben," she said, "It's made it easier for me and you've had a nice day, haven't you?"

"Yes," I replied, as I had had a truly marvellous day at the beach.

"Good boy," she said as she gave me a kiss on the head.

So, it was okay I thought. Apart from the odd teasing by Louise, I'd been wearing a nappy all day and apart from earlier, I wasn't getting into trouble, so that certainly made me happy. Yeah, I had a nappy on, but no one was bothered. Robert was happy, so I thought I'd just enjoy myself.

Blackpool in the '70s.

It was getting late and it was decided we should head back to the guest house. It was still busy and I had enjoyed every minute of it. We soon arrived back at the house and Mrs Williams greeted us.

"Breakfast will be about 8 am," she announced.

We all headed upstairs and into our respective bedrooms. Mum came into mine and said she would be in about five minutes to get me ready for bed.

"That's fine," my auntie replied, "I'll sort him out."

As expected, Sharon wore a nappy for nighttime, so I assumed she'd do me at the same time. My mum kissed me goodnight and headed out of the door leaving Jane, my Auntie, Sharon and I to sort us out.

"Right kiddies," my Auntie said. "It's bedtime."

She went over to the kettle that was in the corner, saying, "I'm dying for a brew!" She switched on the kettle then grabbed a handful of clean nappies off the pile. "Come on you two. On the bed you go."

She laid a towel out and both Sharon and I got up and laid back on the bed. Jane came over and beckoned me to lift my bum as she removed my shorts. It was like a factory. They were both chatting away while Jane was changing my nappy and Sharon was having her night nappy put on. We were both soon ready for bed, freshly nappied and a glass of milk in hand. Night nappies were normal for me, so I didn't feel bad in any way, as this was just routine. Sharon and I got into bed, me in the little camp bed in the corner, and after a short while, the lights were turned out except for a small bedside lamp for Sharon and we drifted off to sleep, exhausted after an absolutely packed and wonderful day.

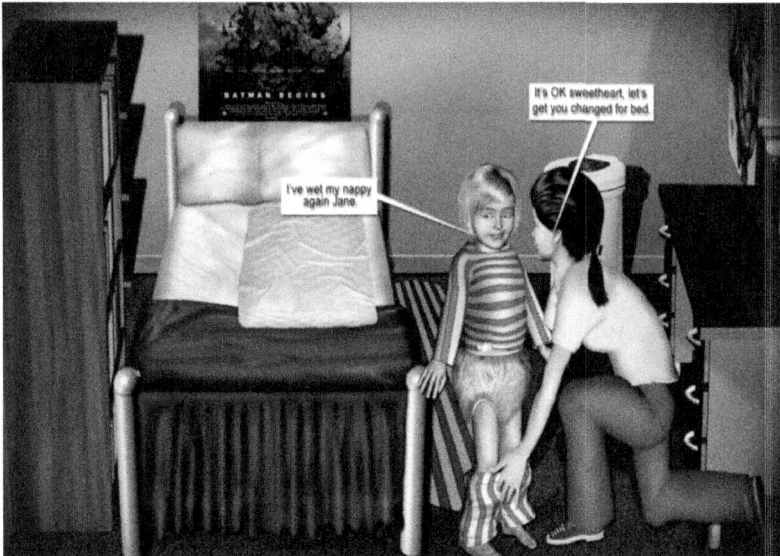

One of the many occasions that Jane changed my nappy

back at the guest house.

Saturday morning arrived and as normal, I woke up and had wet my nappy. Jane and my Auntie were out of the room and as I looked over, Sharon was still asleep. I got out of bed and wandered outside to the landing. I went into mum's room and she was getting ready and helping my brothers get washed and dressed.

"Morning, Ben," she said.

"Morning, mum," I replied.

As I walked over to her, she had a quick feel of my bum and said, "Go back to your room and I'll come and sort you out when I'm ready."

"Okay, mum," and I headed off back to my room.

Sharon had woken up with the opening and closing of the door and sat up in bed asking for her mum. A moment later, Jane and Auntie Karen came in.

"Morning kiddies," they said. "Sleep well?"

Jane then ushered me into the bathroom, took off my wet nappy and stood me in the bath for a hose down! As Jane finished, Auntie Karen came in with Sharon who, like me, was by now only wearing her nappy ready for a change. I walked back into the bedroom wrapped in a towel and Jane dried me off.

My mum walked in and asked if all was going fine. "Yeah, everything's going okay," Jane replied.

"Ah thanks, Jane. You're an angel."

"Is Ben going back in a nappy, Di?"

"Er... Ben," she said, "what do you want to do? I don't want any accidents today, we are out all day, probably."

Jane turned to me and said, "It's fine if you want a nappy on. I'll help you with everything. Not worth worrying, is it?"

"No," I replied, but I was unsure and conflicted about what to do.

After a short time, I agreed to be put into a nappy for the day again. In a way, I was kind of glad, relieved maybe, but I was hoping for one of the disposables, as they were really comfy and didn't feel wet when I used them.

"Can I wear one of the other nappies that Mrs Williams gave us?"

"Er....yeah I suppose so, but I've only got one left. Tell you what, we will put you in that disposable nappy and I'll ask Mrs Williams where they sell them here, and if your mum is okay with it, we will get some more."

"Yeah okay," I replied.

I jumped up on the bed, laid back and Jane came over carrying the white disposable nappy. She opened it up and since yesterday I had forgotten how crinkly it was, but it was comfier, so worth it. She slid the opened nappy under my bum and then asked my Auntie if she had any nappy cream.

She handed Jane a pot of nappy cream and said, "Ben, if we are not careful you will get a nappy rash, it's hot outside and you've been wearing one for a bit now."

She wiped some cream around the necessary areas and then proceeded to bring the nappy between my legs. She taped it into place quite snugly and then lifted me onto the floor. As well as crinkly, it was also a bit bulkier, but at the same time comfier. Jane then helped me on with my t-shirt, and then my shorts which Mrs Williams had now washed and brought back. These were a bit better, as they were larger and went up a lot easier. Socks and trainers on and then we headed off downstairs for breakfast. Everyone was already there, talking and eating cereal. I found an empty seat and sat at the table and poured some milk over my cereal while my mum poured me some juice. It was a nice breakfast, everyone happy and smiling and talking about the day ahead.

As we finished eating, Robert spoke and said, "Right troops! Everyone outside in about fifteen minutes for a nice walk down the promenade."

As instructed, we all went outside, ready to go. My mum asked if I was okay, and with that, she gave Jane some money.

"We will meet you at the cafe in about half an hour," she said to Jane.

Fear and Joy – a life in and out of nappies ❚

Jane took my hand and walked off towards the centre away from the rest of the family.

"I asked your mum," she said. "And Mrs Williams told us where we could buy some more nappies for you, Ben, just for the holiday."

About ten minutes' walk later, we entered into a large supermarket type place, not the ones you have now, but a one-stop convenience store which sold just about everything. We walked up and down the aisles until we came across the baby section. It was filled with everything you could need for a baby or small child on holiday. We went past the terry-towelling nappy shelves and Jane spotted a couple of brands of disposables. I cannot be sure what they were. All I know is that the girls were in a pink packet and the boys in a blue packet.

She looked at the sizes and said to me, "We better get the largest ones I suppose."

With that, she picked up the pack of nappies and headed to the tills. It was probably Pampers, as these are the only type of disposables in a blue carry bag with a baby picture on it that I have been able to find on the internet since.

Jane paid for the nappies and we went on our way. As we walked towards the meeting place, Jane said, "these will be better for you sweetie, won't they."

"Yeah," I replied, feeling unsure and yet pleased about everything.

As we walked, I could feel myself waddling a little and if we were in a quiet area there was a definite tell-tale rustling coming from my direction, but no one had said anything or noticed. We met up with the rest of the family and Jane placed the bag of nappies in Sharon's shelf on her pushchair.

The disposable nappies that I used from Mrs Williams were

the same as these!

The day pretty much went as a day out at the seaside normally does. We all had great fun, walking on the beach, going to arcades, buying stuff at souvenir shops and having a great time as a family. I only needed one change during the day, which my mum very expertly did, even though she had never put on a disposable nappy before.

She did say though, "Don't get used to these. I can't afford to throw away nappies, young man. Once these have run out, its back to your normal ones."

I suppose I had a better day than normal too. I didn't worry about having accidents, which meant nobody got mad or upset with me and I was able to enjoy the day care-free, albeit with a bulky bum and I rustled like a crisp packet at times. Jane did as she said she would and checked often if I needed the loo and also had a quick check of the nappy to make sure it wasn't too wet, but at least she did it inconspicuously, which was a relief as there were lots and lots of people about.

As tea time approached, we wandered back towards the guest house where our evening meal had been prepared for us. We were all so hungry after the packed day we had just had, and I don't think a single bit of food was left. Once we were all fed and watered, we made our way to the lounge area where the adults sat drinking tea and having a smoke. We kids made use of the few toys that were lying about. Robert then announced that he was taking my mum out for a drink and Auntie Karen and Janet were in charge.

"Right kiddies, what shall we do?" Janet announced. Arcades, beach and lots of other shrieks were called out by us all. "Right then, let's go upstairs and put some clean clothes on and we will decide."

We all raced upstairs into our respective bedrooms. Janet told my brothers to wait in her room with Louise and Josh while she got some things out of mum's room. Jane, Auntie Karen, Sharon and I went into our room. My Auntie came over and did what most people did when checking if I had wet myself and so on - stand over me, pull my shorts away and have a quick feel of my nappy.

"Hmm," came the reply, "We might as well change this nappy now if we are going out."

Quick as a flash, she pulled down my shorts, untaped my wet nappy and asked Jane to bring in a wet flannel. After a quick, harsh wipe down and dry, I laid down on the changing mat which she had placed on the floor. She grabbed a cloth nappy and plastic pants and proceeded to fold it ready to place on me.

Thankfully, Jane quickly said, "Is he not better in one of the disposable ones if going out Karen? I think they are comfier for him."

"Pass me one then," she said as she threw the terry nappy on the bed and placed the rustling disposable under my bum.

I was a bit embarrassed now as Sharon stood next to her watching me, no nappy on and yet here was me, nearly six years old and still getting my nappy changed! No sooner was I taped in a dry nappy and my shorts pulled up, I was ushered out of the door. We all proceeded to the beach which was only a short stroll away. The tide was slowly going out and my Auntie said we could paddle in the shallow water. We left our trainers and socks with Auntie Karen and Janet and we ran down to the water's edge and dipped our toes in. Even though it was warm air, the water was freezing and we were all giggling and laughing as we put our feet in the water then running back out. It was great. We were so lucky to be here and have never experienced the seaside before, it was just sheer joy.

About half an hour passed, and we were called up to get our socks and shoes on again. We then headed back onto the promenade and towards the ice cream shop we visited the previous night. After ice creams and a drink, we ventured to the arcades where again we were given some loose change to play on the machines. We had all soon spent everything and were back out walking up the promenade listening to all the machines and smelling the fast food being cooked. We were soon very tired.

Josh was asleep in his pushchair and Sharon and my younger brother were complaining they were tired, so we headed back to the guest house. As usual, Mrs Williams was there to greet us and ask us if we had had a good time. She then said that she would make warm milk for the kids once we were in our pyjamas and cups of tea for the grownups. We all rushed upstairs and got undressed with the grown-ups wandering between each room supervising. Jane was helping Janet, so Sharon and I were left with my Auntie.

"Get undressed, Ben," she asked. By the time I had removed my shoes, socks, shorts and t-shirt she had lifted Sharon onto the bed and was putting her nappy on. "I won't be long Ben, just wait there for me."

Janet then entered the room and said, "Hello Ben! Don't you look like a big boy with a posh nappy on?"

I smiled and didn't know what to think or say, so I just agreed. Maybe she was right. Maybe these did make me look like a big boy. Soon I was lifted onto the bed and laid back so that my Auntie could sort me out. As she went to undo the tapes she had noticed that I hadn't used it yet as it had only been a couple of hours since I had been changed.

"Good boy," she said. "See, you can do it. Do you need a wee now?"

"Yeah," I replied.

She picked me up and ushered me to the bathroom, where she managed to sit me on the toilet and pull my nappy up and away, allowing me to wee into the toilet. Once I'd finished, she straightened my nappy back out and told me to go back to the room. Once in there, she came over with my pyjamas and a pair of plastic pants.

"Put these on over the top, Ben. I'm not sure if this nappy will last all night without leaking."

With that, I stepped into the pants and they were pulled up over my disposable nappy. Pyjamas and slippers on, we all then went downstairs to drink our milk and eat a couple of biscuits she had also left out for us.

Heaven, absolute heaven this was!

We were allowed to play for a few minutes more before we were all tucked up in bed, lights out and sound asleep, having had a very long and action-packed day.

No sooner had I closed my eyes when I was woken by my mum telling me it was time to get up. My Auntie, Sharon and Jane had been up for about an hour and had been downstairs while my brothers, Louise and I had all still been asleep. We were exhausted from the previous night and had all slept the night through. I followed my mum on to the landing, where she told me to go downstairs to the dining room where breakfast had been prepared.

As I walked down the stairs, I became aware that my nappy was absolutely soaked. Not surprising really, as I hadn't woken up at all during the night and if it were not for the plastic pants my auntie had made me put on, I dare say it would have fallen down! It made a really loud crinkling noise too, much worse than it normally did and I couldn't understand why, although I do now!

As I walked into the dining area, I said good morning, and everyone responded back. I made a beeline for the nearest vacant seat and sat down as quickly as I could. I was very conscious about the state I was in even though everyone knew I would be wearing a nappy. The disposable made it quite obvious due to the crisp packet sound they made every time I moved. I was not as comfortable as usual as I sat there. Every time I moved, I didn't like the feeling that I was becoming aware of in my pyjamas. The wadding or whatever they were made of in those days had bound together and were in small clumps and not evenly as distributed as they were when dry and fresh. It was a wonderful thing that my Auntie had decided to make me wear 'just in case' plastic pants, as I'm sure this nappy would have come off in the night otherwise, as I was known to be a mover and wriggler in my sleep. However, I was so hungry that I just ate my cornflakes, scoffed two slices of toast and drank down a beaker of fruit juice trying to ignore my saturated behind for a bit.

As soon as we finished breakfast, we all went upstairs to get ready for our last full day at the seaside. It was Sunday and we were heading home on Monday afternoon. Mum came into my room and took my soaked nappy off, commenting that it was a good idea of Auntie Karen's to use the pants over the top. I had a quick wash down in the bathtub then was placed in a towel to dry off while she went and got my younger brother ready and herself.

Jane came in and said she would help me shortly once she had done the final preparation of her daily routine. I sat on my bed, colouring in the book I had bought the previous day with not a care in the world. To be honest, it felt weird just sitting there with no nappy on. For the previous two and a half days, I had been in a nappy all the time, only out of it temporarily during changes and washes. Anyway, I gladly sat there while the sun beamed through the opened windows and lots of activity ensued in the room.

Fear and Joy – a life in and out of nappies ▌

Sharon, as usual, had been taken out of her bedtime nappy and was now wearing proper girl knickers and her outfit for the day. Soon it was my turn and up onto the bed I climbed and laid back for Jane to sort me out. Thankfully, she came with a disposable nappy and by now had gotten quite good at putting them on. She slid it under my bum then pulled the nappy through my legs, opened it up and taped it perfectly into place, having a smile and talking to me nicely all the while. I was then lifted onto the floor where she helped me on with my shorts, as I could never get my shorts over any type of nappy. I then picked my t-shirt for the day out, put it on and then Jane sat me on the bed while she fastened my trainers. Again, the subtle crisp packet sound echoed from beneath my shorts, but at least I knew they'd be comfortable all day and I would not have to worry.

We were all soon gathered in the hallway and heading out towards the promenade. The adults all had bags with swim kit, sandwiches, drinks and more, as today was a beach day. The weather was amazing, hot and sunny. As we walked down the footpath, the familiar sounds and smells soon hit us. We were soon on the promenade and crossing over towards the beach. You could smell the sea and hear it. Along with all the other kids, I was very excited. As usual, my mind was soon distracted from my nappy clad bum and I just went about my normal routine. It was still however harder to walk in a disposable, as they were much thicker than a terry-towelling one, but comfier at the same time. I'm sure any parent that noticed the tell-tale bulge of my front and bum inside my shorts would not have to guess twice at what this little chappy had on under his shorts.

We found a good spot on the sand and a few towels were laid down for us and we were told to take our socks and shoes off. I grabbed my bucket and spade and started to build sandcastles and the other kids were doing the same. It was such a beautiful day. The beach was very, very busy and everyone who I could hear or see were clearly having a fantastic time as well. Robert was sunbathing in his shorts only and mum laid down next to him, also sunbathing while keeping a check on the kids in turn with Auntie Karen and Janet. Jane was actively engaged with us, building in the sand and helping bring seawater from the sea to fill the moats. It was so good to be doing this on such a lovely day. Normally, we would either be in the back yard or playing in the back alleyway which was good, but nowhere near as good as this.

As the day grew warmer and sunnier we were doused in sun cream. Mum took my t-shirt off and applied it liberally all over my upper body and legs as she did the same to my two brothers who then carried on playing. I too just went back to my sandcastles and continued to build my masterpiece. I hadn't realised that by now, having no t-shirt on and just a pair of shorts, the waistband of my nappy had decided to make an appearance! Of course, I could still hear it when I moved, but I'd been in them for ages now, so had gotten used to it.

As I walked down to the sea, only about twenty metres or so, some people were looking at me and I just thought they were just being nosey or curious, so I just carried on walking. A couple of kids were giggling as they do and pointing, but again I just ignored it, thinking it was nothing to do with me. I got to the sea, filled my bucket and returned to my sandcastle where I poured the water in and watched it move around the moat I had built. Just as I stood up and was about to go back to get some more water, mum beckoned me to come over to her. As soon as I reached her, she knelt up and pulled up my shorts and readjusted the nappy, which I now realised was on view and probably what people had seen and the kids had been giggling at. She noticed that my nappy had become a bit wet, and although I had been able to use the toilet on one occasion, I had done a couple of small wees into my nappy as I was allowed to.

"Lie on the towel, Ben," my mum said in a quiet voice.

No sooner had I laid down, mum pulled my shorts down and untaped my nappy. She quickly put a clean one under my bum and pulled it through my legs, taping it into place. This was done in lightning quick time, not something she would have able to do with a terry nappy. My shorts were then pulled back up, my nappy tucked in as best as she could, and with that, she patted my bum.

"There you go. All done," and with that, I went back to playing.

I suppose as it was done quickly, I never got a chance to think who might have been watching me having my nappy changed on the middle of the beach. No one had made a fuss or anything - so I didn't either. I must admit though, even at that young age, having a clean nappy put on felt so much better and I soon realised just how wet the nappy that had just been removed truly was. I didn't go back to the sea to get some water, as I now knew what some of the people were staring at and some kids giggling at. Of course, there were other kids just playing with just a nappy on, but they were young toddler age kids, which no one took any notice of, but I was a normal-sized boy for my age and still wearing a nappy. I'm not surprised really. It knocked my confidence a bit and I refused to move away from our camp area as, although my shorts had been sorted and I could have pulled them up myself if it happened again, I didn't want to take the chance, so I was happy enough just sitting and playing with Josh, Sharon and Janet.

Janet could tell I was a little bit subdued. "What's up, honey?"

"Nothing," I said.

"Come on, tell me what's up."

I told her what had happened, and she just put her arm around me and said, "It doesn't matter sweetheart, don't take any notice of what other people say or do. It's not your fault is it, and you're having a better day not worrying, aren't you?"

"Yes," I replied, "But people can tell that I'm wearing a nappy and I'm too old."

"You're not too old, sweetheart. Other children older than you wear nappies and that's not their fault either. Look, let's put your t-shirt back on and then no one can see".

"Yes please," I replied with great relief.

With that, she grabbed my t-shirt and helped me on with it. I was now happier to go back to the sea and get some more water. I did ask Janet to come with me - which she did - as Jane could watch Sharon and Josh.

Playing on the beach and I didn't know my nappy was

showing. No one was bothered though, except me!

As the afternoon wore on, we were all having such a great day, and everyone was laughing. Even Robert cracked a few laughs during the day, but soon we were all told to come back to the towels and get all our things together, as tea would be served soon at the guest house. We all walked off the beach, smiling and chatting and headed the short distance to our guest house. On arrival, Mrs Williams greeted us all with tea, coffee and squash for us kids. As usual, she gave us a little treat by way of a chocolate biscuit and explained to the adults that tea would be a little later than normal, so we had time to get freshened up if we like. With that, we all went upstairs and into our rooms where we told each other our little bits of snippets from the day that others might not have seen or known about.

While we waited for the tea to be ready, I jumped up onto Jane's bed. Hers was a bit comfier to sit on, as it had a headboard whereas mine didn't. Jane joined me and we laughed and giggled about the day, telling each other things that we had seen and so on. I even said that mum had changed my nappy on the beach and that nobody said anything.

"I know she did! I saw you and you were very grown-up about it, weren't you? And I told you nobody notices, didn't I, you silly billy."

I laughed with her and she started to tickle me. My Auntie joined in and within a minute both Sharon and I were being tickled so much we couldn't breathe for laughing. I liked Jane and I know she liked me and my brothers. She never complained, even when changing nappies several times a day. She always smiled and laughed and very rarely raised her voice at us. I often wonder what happened to her, but I never got to find out.

Mrs Williams soon beckoned us downstairs for our tea. We all raced downstairs and into the dining area which had been set the same as always. As it was Sunday, we were served a massive roast dinner followed by cake and custard. It was absolutely delicious, and everyone cleared their plates. I think the sea air and all the playing all day had made us that bit hungrier. Mrs Williams then said if we would like to go to the lounge, she would bring the adults tea, coffee and juice for the kids. We went into the lounge and again played with the few toys that were in there. Robert read the paper and the ladies chatted.

"Well, it's our last night in Blackpool, everyone. What shall we do?" Robert asked us.

After about five minutes of shouted suggestions and hoping for their idea to be chosen, we were told to be ready to go out in about half an hour.

"Right kids. Come on, let's go and get you all cleaned up," said mum.

We all ran upstairs and waited for our clean clothes to be given to us.

"I'll sort Ben out, Di,", Jane said, as she walked into our room past my mum's.

"Ok love, thanks."

"Right, squidgy bum. Come here." She chased me around the room and soon grabbed hold of me and playfully threw me onto the bed. "Right young man, let's get a clean nappy on for going out okay?"

"Yeeeah…" I screamed at her.

I was getting used to this by now and so was everybody else. I laid back so she could start the routine. Jane pulled off my shorts and then proceeded to untape my nappy, pulling it from underneath me. She folded it up and placed it on the floor and reached for the flannel my auntie had used on Sharon. As soon as she had washed and dried me, she applied a liberal amount of cream to the necessary areas and sprinkled a small amount of talcum powder onto my bum. She unfolded the disposable nappy and slid it underneath me, stopping in the perfect place to bring the nappy up through my legs. She was getting good at this now. She taped it into position and then asked my Auntie for a pair of plastic pants. I didn't question it. I just raised my feet and she fed them through the holes and pulled the pants up to my bum before lifting each side and pulling the pants into position. She made sure all the nappy was tucked inside the nappy pants and then lifted me down onto the floor.

As she pulled my shorts up, she said, "It's okay if you use your nappy while we are out sweetie. That's why I've put your nappy pants on. Don't worry about asking to go to the toilet. I'll tell your mum that I'll get you ready for bed when we get back okay. Just enjoy your night, Ben and forget about having accidents. Your nappy won't leak, and I'll let mum know about it all."

"Yes, but I won't get into trouble will I, Jane?"

"No, no. Of course, you won't. It's just easier for me and your mum if we don't have to take your nappy off when you need a wee. We can have more time having fun, rather than queuing to go to the toilet, can't we?"

"Ok Jane," I said quietly.

I was still a little bit wary of being told to use my nappy whenever I wanted to, but at that age, you just do as you're told. I was soon fully dressed with trainers on and ready to go out.

My Auntie spoke to Jane and said, "That's a good idea for Ben. I might put Sharon in one as it's getting late." She called Sharon over and asked her, "Sharon do you want your nappy on now like Ben?"

"No, no!" Sharon objected and so my auntie agreed, and we then headed back out onto the promenade.

As we turned onto the promenade I thought to myself this is my last night here and felt a bit sad. It had been a great time though and I hoped I would come back again. We soon got the aroma of candy floss, burgers and seafood, but having had such a large tea, we all just walked past them. No one, not even any of us kids asked for sweets or anything! Robert then told us our last night was going to be spent at the 'pleasure beach'.

We hadn't been up till now as even then it was quite expensive, but Robert to my great surprise said, "You've all been really good, so it's my treat for all of you kids!".

We all screamed out appreciation – even Jane. I ran up to Robert to give him a hug and say thank you.

"It's alright, Ben. You're welcome," he said. "Even you've been good, haven't you?"

"Yes," I replied.

At that moment I thought to myself it was worth wearing a nappy all the time while here, as not once did I get shouted at for wetting myself or constantly asking to go to the toilet. The pleasure beach was soon in sight and the last fifty metres or so we all ran towards the entrance and were just amazed at how big the place was.

It was about 7 o'clock and was still quite busy, but it was the right time to go as there were no queues at each ride. As we walked around, we wanted to go on different rides. As expected, some of us were old enough or tall enough and some of us weren't. We were soon passing the toilets and as normal, mum asked if anyone wanted to go before we ventured too far in. Most went, but as Jane had said earlier, I was okay to use my nappy if I wanted to.

Jane came over and told me my mum had said she was okay with what she had suggested and with that she started trying to tickle me as I was wriggling, trying to get out of her grasp. Next thing I knew, I was upside down over her shoulder laughing hard, as we waited for the others to come out of the toilets. She then turned me over and held me up with her arms around my bum and made funny faces at me. I don't know why, but I just let go of my bladder and started to wee into my nappy. It felt great not having to go into a dirty toilet and have my nappy pulled down and then try and find a clean place to lie or sit down while it was either taped or pinned on again. To me, it was so much easier and with wearing a disposable nappy, it wasn't quite as bad a feeling. As they all exited the loos, Jane put me down and took my hand and we all walked towards the rides.

Mum was soon at my side and said, "You okay, love?"

"Yeah mum," I replied with a wide smile. I really was very okay.

Our first ride was a small one so that most of us could go on. It was a kind of mini roller coaster. I sat with my younger brother, and Janet got on with Sharon. It was fantastic. Around and around we went, laughing and giggling as you do. It was soon over though, and we headed over to the bigger rides for my older brother and Louise, who decided on the dodgems for some reason. As the ride stopped, they ran onto the floor and grabbed a car each. Not many people were on and the ride attendant was beckoning more of us in.

"He's too small!" shouted my mum, pointing to me.

"It's fine if an adult goes in with him!" the attendant shouted back.

So, mum and I jumped in one car together and joined the other two. As soon as the ride started we were whizzing round, crashing into other cars. Mum then asked if I wanted to drive.

"Yeah!" I screamed.

With that, I took the wheel and headed for Louise... revenge time for taking the Mickey out of me wearing nappies.

I managed a slight clip of her car and then was rammed by my brother. I suppose, funnily enough, this was the first time I drove while wearing a nappy and like before, it helped with the hard seats and when jolted up and back down into the seats, it definitely cushioned my bum, so I was on a winner again. Once the ride was over, we headed over to the cafe area, so we could get a drink.

It was about 8 o'clock by then, yet it was still very warm and we were all really thirsty. As we sat down, Jane sat next to me and did a quick nappy check. Only this time instead of the back as it was usually done, she pulled my shorts down just a bit at the front and had a feel and look at the front. I didn't care. I just carried on what I was doing, really not bothered in the slightest what was being done. I later found out that if my terry nappy was wet or starting to get wet at the back then it was probably soaked at the front so time for a change. However, since disposable nappies were much more absorbent, it would be hard to tell just from looking at the back of a nappy.

"Have you had a wee wee, Ben?" she enquired.

"Yes," I replied, but this time not in an ashamed voice as was common for me.

She gently pulled my shorts up to cover my nappy and we both carried on having a drink of pop. It was nice having Jane looking after me now and again. It was a change for me from the normal routine that mums get into. I think Jane enjoyed looking after smaller kids and with me being a bit older and able to kind or sort myself out, she had the best of both worlds - nappies to deal with and still able to have a bit more fun than looking after a smaller baby. This didn't bother me at all. I had known Jane for as long as I could remember, and she was more like a sister. It was soon getting late, so not long after our drink, we all got together and headed back to the guest house for our last night having had fun on a few rides and playing 'hook a duck' and so on at the pleasure beach.

As we entered the guest house, Mrs Williams greeted us and stated that hot milk for the kids and tea and coffee for the adults would be ready in about ten minutes. We made our way to the lounge where we chatted and laughed about our time at the pleasure beach and our day in general. Milk and biscuits finished, all the kids were told to go upstairs and get their pyjamas on. I looked at Jane and as promised, she accompanied me, as she said she would, to help me get ready for bed. I was glad as well, as I had been using my nappy most of the night and it was probably soaking. It felt fine, but that was only because it was one of those disposable type nappies and not my normal terry-towelling ones. I jumped up on the bed and lay back in readiness for the nappy change.

Jane pulled my trainers off then pulled my shorts down revealing a very wet nappy! She just smiled as always and no sooner had she pulled off my plastic pants, she was un-taping the nappy and folding it up, placing it on the side. She got a wet flannel and soap, cleaned me all over then walked over to the shelf and picked up one of my regular fluffy white towelling nappies, plastic pants and a pair of white nappy pins. She slid the nappy under my bum, applied some talcum powder then expertly pinned it into place with two locking nappy pins. I lifted my feet and she eased the pants over my feet, one leg at a time, then pulled them up as far as she could. She then lifted one leg and pulled up the pants on one side over my nappy, then onto the other side, finally pulling the front then back evenly into place. She made sure the entire nappy was contained within the plastic pants and then pulled me up and put on my pyjama tops and bottoms.

"Right sweetie. All done. Shall we go back down for a bit until bedtime?"

"Sure!" I replied, and I waddled out of our room with Jane, while my Auntie got Sharon ready.

Sharon was being difficult and didn't want her nappy on much to my Auntie Karen's annoyance. I'd enjoyed having mine put on a few times this holiday and this was one of them. Jane was so kind to me and I really liked her for it.

Blackpool in the '70s.

We were allowed to play in the lounge for a bit longer as it was our last night at the guest house. Mrs Williams joined us and was having a drink with the adults. She had been a lovely host and had looked after us all really well during our stay. I can't count the number of nappies she must have washed for us, but it would have been quite a few over the weekend. My mum called me over and lifted me onto her knee.

"What do you say, Ben, to Mrs Williams for helping us?"

"Thank you, Mrs Williams," I replied.

As she had done most of the washing for me, I was the spokesperson for the kids I think.

"You're welcome, my little sweet. I hope you've had a good time here!"

My mum pulled me back into her body and put her arms around my waist and kissed my head lovingly. She was patting the front of my shorts like mothers do and which she also did at home when I had got ready for bed at night and was sitting on her knee watching TV.

"Are you ok now, love? Did Jane change your nappy for you?"

"Yeah, she did, mum. I like Jane, mum."

She turned around and thanked Jane and lifted me off her knee telling me to go and give Jane a hug for looking after me so well. I ran over to Jane who swept me off my feet and sat me in her lap. With her arms around me, I felt so safe and loved. It was soon time for bed and we all went upstairs to our rooms where we got into bed and waited for mum to come and kiss us goodnight. It was our last sleep at this wonderful guest house. As I lay there, Sharon was mumbling to Auntie Karen and Jane was reading a magazine of some kind. I sat up and asked Jane if I could sleep in her bed tonight.

"Of course, you can, Ben. Come on in."

She swept back the covers and I jumped into bed. I lay there looking at the pictures in her magazine while Jane was trying to tell me what they were about. I must have soon drifted off to sleep as the next time I woke up, it was dark, and everyone was asleep. I turned over and noticed that Jane was fast asleep, so I shut my eyes and drifted back to sleep myself. It was soon morning and I woke up and realised Jane wasn't there. She soon returned and said she had been downstairs for a drink.

"Did you sleep well, Ben?"

"Mmm," I replied groggily.

She sat back on the bed and gave me a cuddle and said it was too early to get up yet as everyone was still asleep. She put her arm around me and I soon fell asleep again. It was about 9 am when I was woken up by my Auntie, telling me to get out of bed, as breakfast was being prepared downstairs. As I stumbled out of bed, I had, as usual, soaked my nappy and it was sagging a bit, but I didn't care. I just put my slippers on and went downstairs and found a vacant seat to sit in.

Breakfast wasn't the same this morning, probably because we knew we were heading home later that day, but we were still all chatting about what we were going to do that morning till it was time to set off. As soon as we had finished breakfast, we were all told by Robert to go and get ready and make sure we had packed our stuff ready to go in the car. There was a lot of movement that morning, people rushing from room to room, grabbing stuff off each other and trying to pack as best they could quickly so we could enjoy the last day. Jane was also busy packing the small case she had brought, so I just looked about for any toys or stuff that belonged to me and took them into mum's room where she had collected all the washing from Mrs Williams and was trying to sort out what each of us would wear for the day.

I walked into my room where Auntie Karen was busy packing and for the first time ever, I had to ask for my nappy to be changed! Normally, I would be told when I would be changed, but as everyone was busy, I was still in my night nappy and couldn't get dressed until I was sorted. I had assumed that I was going to be put back into a nappy for the day, so I tugged at Jane and asked if she could change my nappy.

"Of course, sweet. Just give me a minute and I'll get you sorted".

Just then, mum walked in. "Take your pyjamas off, Ben," she demanded.

I pulled my top off and then my bottoms and stood there in just my nappy, waiting for either mum or Jane to do the next bit. Louise then walked in with a toy that belonged to Sharon which Josh had been playing with. She immediately noticed me just wandering around.

"Haha, nappy bum, you've got a baby nappy on," she remarked in a childish way.

"Louise!", my Auntie quickly replied. "Don't be so horrible to Ben".

"But he has though, and he shouldn't be wearing nappies at his age! Sharon doesn't!"

"That's not the point, Louise. Ben can't help it and he's not harming anyone, so what's the problem?"

My mum called me from her bedroom to come to her room. As I was only wearing a nappy I can remember trying to ignore her. There were too many people flying about the place and no way was I walking out on the landing like this.

"Ben!" came the shout again. "Come here now".

Louise then took great delight saying, "Ben, your mum's calling you. He's coming, auntie Di!"

I gave her an angry look and then proceeded into the corridor towards my mum's room. I remember thinking that I'd get my own back for her doing that. As I headed my mum's room, Mrs Williams was coming up the stairs.

"Hello dear!" she said, "I've just got the last bits of washing for your mum, where is she?"

I pointed to where my mum was, and I followed her in.

"Ah thank you," mum said, as she grabbed the last few items. "I'll take last night's nappies home but thank you so much for washing the others over the weekend."

"It's my pleasure. I'll see you before you go."

As Mrs Williams left the room, Robert came out of the bathroom having just had a shave.

"You're dressed for the day then, boy?" he said, looking at me standing there with no clothes on.

My mum turned around. "Ben," she said. "When Jane has taken that nappy off, put it in this bag and bring it back to me."

I think she assumed that Jane would have sorted me by now and was just going to give me a bag and instruct me to go and get the nappy Jane had just taken off me.

"Tell Jane to put you in a disposable nappy today, then I don't have to find more bags later. Hurry up, as I want to pack it".

I returned to the room with the carrier bag and handed it to Jane telling her what my mum had just said to me.

"Okay sweetie," she replied. "Go and grab a nappy and I'll change you now."

I grabbed a nappy out of the packet and handed it to Jane who lifted me on the bed and proceeded in her own loving way to remove the very wet nappy and put me in a fresh comfy disposable one with a clean pair of plastic pants so that it would last a while. She then put the cloth nappy in the bag along with the used plastic pants and I gave it to my mum, so she could pack it. As I walked along the corridor and into mum's room, the normal crisp—packet-like sound hit me, but at least no one was around to see or hear me. I opened mum's door and handed her the heavy bag containing the wet cloth nappy.

"Good boy. Well done!" she said. "Now go and get dressed. We are going to be leaving in about half an hour."

I returned to my room as Janet turned towards me and said, "Doesn't he look so cute just walking about with his new style nappy on?"

It was said in a loving and motherly sort of way towards me, so I just smiled at her, but at the same time, I felt a little embarrassed. I was soon dressed and we all trooped down the stairs with our bags and cases and headed out into the car park where they were expertly place in by Robert... a man thing! We were all then instructed to go back inside and thank Mrs Williams for having us and so on. We went into the entrance hall and said goodbye, we kids giving her a hug and the adults a kiss on the cheek and handshakes and so forth. She said we were okay until one pm to leave the car on the driveway, which gave us about three hours or so.

Fear and Joy – a life in and out of nappies ▌

We decided to walk on the beach, taking in the smells, sights and sounds for one last time before going home to smoky Manchester. We were told to stay away from the water and only play on the dry sand which we did and built a few sandcastles and generally just played about. The adults sat on the sea wall keeping an eye on us. Janet had taken Josh for a walk in his pushchair, as he was playing up a bit. It was getting hot though and it was only mid-morning. As it drew towards dinner time, we headed to our favourite cafe and had a small snack and drink for lunch. It was now time to head back to the car, so mum asked if anyone wanted a wee which, as usual, most did so off they trotted while I got the now-obligatory nappy check. I had already used it a couple of times, but not for big wees, just enough to make me not want a wee.

"You'll be fine till we get home love," mum said, and she pulled my shorts up. They weren't all the way down, just enough for her to gain access to check my nappy easily.

We headed back towards the car where we all climbed in and headed off back home to Manchester. It was not long before we were in traffic and we had only gone halfway down the promenade. I didn't care how long we were stuck in traffic as I had a nappy on so could go for a wee when I wanted, which was a great feeling, as I didn't need to worry about accidents.

We soon hit the motorway and we could go a bit faster, although it was still very busy. I sat back in my seat, got my colouring book out and then as I was getting to the point of needing to go to the loo, I just let go and started weeing in my nappy. These disposable nappies were great for me at the time. Although it was wet, it felt okay and not as bad as when I had terry ones on. I moved my bum a bit to make myself comfy again and continued to colour in my book. My younger brother was soon whimpering that he needed a wee.

"Haha. Not laughing at me, now are you?" I thought silently, as I did another little wee, just because I could.

"Hold onto it, Alex. There's a good boy," my mum said.

Robert then piped up, "I'll be stopping soon lad. Not long now."

If that was me, he would have been complaining about me having to use the toilet again but didn't say anything about Alex needing a wee. About fifteen minutes later, we pulled into a garage area and Robert found a parking spot.

"Come on kids," mum said as she got out of the car.

They headed for the toilet and I stayed with Robert. Robert shouted at my mum to be quick, as he wanted to go for a coffee. There was a small cafe at the side of the garage with tables outside.

"Okay," she shouted back.

"I suppose you've used your nappy, haven't you?" Robert spat out. "Are you not embarrassed at your age still wearing those bloody things? Not fair on your mum, is it?"

"No," I replied sullenly.

"All weekend you've been wearing nappies and peeing yourself. You're just very lazy in my opinion. I'd have had you walking around with them on show. That would have made you learn quickly to use the toilet like the rest of us. It's a good job Jane was with us, Ben. Your mum needed a break as well as the rest of us and you didn't help to have to be changed five times a day."

He exaggerated on that score, but it still made me feel ashamed.

"Sorry," I said, feeling deeply embarrassed.

"No good being sorry, Ben. Grow up and stop being so bloody lazy and needing nappies all the time. I think you do it on purpose to get attention. Well, it doesn't wash with me."

Thankfully, mum returned with my brothers and I could escape the tirade of hurtful comments from Robert. I don't think he liked me and to be honest, I never liked him much either. Mum asked if I was okay, as she said I had a sad face.

"Do you need your nappy changed, Ben?" She pulled my shorts down a bit and discovered I had used my nappy several times.

"Jane, can you change Ben's nappy while I go with Robert to the cafe and order some drinks?"

"Yeah course, Di," she answered.

We went towards the toilet, but Jane couldn't find a suitable place to change me, so we headed back to the cars where Jane got a blanket out of the boot and laid it on the back seat of Janet's car and proceeded to change me. She couldn't find the bag with a couple of disposables left, so she got a cloth nappy out and proceeded to pin that on me, followed by the same pair of plastic pants.

"There you go!" she exclaimed with a beaming smile, as she stood me up and put my shorts back on.

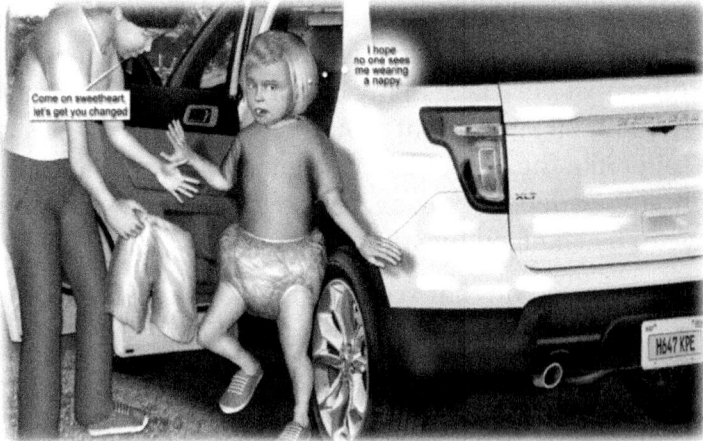

Getting my nappy changed on the way home!

Thankfully, no one was around. That would have been embarrassing having my nappy changed in a garage forecourt. We headed over to the cafe where everyone else was and I sat as far away from Robert as I could.

He looked at me and then out loud said to Jane, "Have you changed the baby's nappy?"

Jane looked as embarrassed as I did. He'd never said anything the whole time at Blackpool, so why now?

Thankfully my mum spoke in my defence. "Robert, don't have a go at him. He can't help it, and it's no problem."

I just sat there and looked down and had a bite of my cake and hoped he wouldn't say anything else to me.

"He needs to learn, Di. It's not right! He's six years old and still wearing bloody nappies. What's wrong with him?"

"Nothing," my mum replied quietly. "He will get himself right soon, won't you Ben?"

I didn't say anything in case I said the wrong thing. Thankfully, my brother spilt his drink and attention was turned to him and away from me. I just sat there and kept quiet, hoping not to attract any more attention from Robert. We were soon heading back towards home.

The rest of the journey I spent in a quiet way just looking out of the window, enjoying the views. Whereas before I could have a little laugh at my brothers needing a wee as I had a nappy on and could use it, they were now laughing *at* me. My older brother taking great delight in pulling back my shorts and plastic pants waist elastic then letting it go. I decided that the best thing to do was to sit back and open my colouring book and ignore them.

As we neared home, I could see the familiar sights of Manchester. Smoke rising from the chimneys and compared to Blackpool, dull grey streets. As we pulled outside our house, my next-door neighbours emerged from their houses, waving excitedly. My mum opened her door and they all began nattering about how the holiday went and was it nice and so on.

"Come on kids. Out of the car."

I was last to get out and I tried as hard as I could to get to the front door without anyone seeing me, as normally I only wore a nappy at night. I had no chance as the gate was still shut, which I couldn't reach to open. The adults were still talking while Robert emptied the boot. Louise took great delight in staring at me and pointing out to the other kids to look at me. I knew them all as we played in the back alleys and on the street outside the house and a couple I went to school with.

"You've got a nappy on Ben," one shouted. The others then joined in and laughed.

As soon as the gate and door were opened, I dashed into the house, so no one could see me anymore. Mum soon came in and told me to take my bag upstairs and that she would come and sort me out in a while. I was hoping that this meant she would take me out of nappies now and put me back in underpants. A little time passed, and I had put my toys away and was messing about with some of my other toys when mum came into my bedroom.

"Come with me, Ben. Let's get you sorted."

I followed her into her bedroom and she picked me up, put me on the bed and told me to lie back. I hoped now that the day nappies were ending.

Mum then spoke in a kind of stern parenting tone and said, "Ben, you're six now, not four and we need to stop this nappy wearing and wetting. Robert is right. I know I told you to use them, but I shouldn't have had to say this in the first place, should I?"

"No mum, I'm sorry. I won't wee anymore I promise."

"We are going to have to get a bit stricter with this Ben, otherwise you're never going to learn," she said sternly. "I'm sorry Ben, but you can stay in a nappy for the rest of the day. You had an accident on Friday when I took you out of nappies in Blackpool remember? And I want a nice easy rest of the day, as Robert is staying till tomorrow. Okay?"

She was right, no sooner had she taken me out of nappies when we got to Blackpool, I had wet myself on the beach, so I've only myself to blame. Maybe it would happen again. So, on the one hand, I was relieved I was staying in a nappy, but at the same time anxious, as I'd have to play outside with it on. So, with all this decided, mum pulled down my plastic pants and undid my nappy. It was only a bit wet, but she decided to change it anyway. As usual, she grabbed a dry nappy, lifted my bum up and slid it under my bum then brought it between my legs. She grabbed the nappy pins, one in her mouth and proceeded to pin the nappy in place. Then she pulled up my plastic pants making sure no cloth was poking out of the elastics on my legs and waist. She then helped me put my shorts back on and then told me to put my trainers back on and go back downstairs.

As I walked out of the bedroom, I got that anxious feeling back again, as I knew that all the kids would know that I've been put into a nappy again. Walking down the stairs, impending fear came over me, as I thought it's only early afternoon and I'm going to be like this until the next day.

I wouldn't play outside, as I didn't want to be seen like this by the other kids, whereas before, it never bothered me. Instead, I headed to the front lounge and got some toys out of the box and started to play with them instead of going outside. I had been in there about fifteen minutes when my mum came in.

"Go and play outside in the back-yard Ben. You're not stopping in on a day like this."

"No!" I replied. "People will laugh at me!"

"No, they won't, come on love. Go outside and enjoy yourself."

I got up and walked through the kitchen and out into the back yard where my brothers were playing along with Steve's friend. As I sat on the concrete floor playing with my outdoor toys, I hoped no one would see me or say anything, but at least I had my shorts on. They all soon went into the back-alley way to play, leaving me on my own with my younger brother. I remained like this for the rest of the day.

Occasionally, my mum would come out and ask me if I needed the toilet. If I did, she would pull my nappy down and put me on the loo, then refasten it when I'd finished.

The alleyway where we played at the rear of our house

I stayed in nappies during the day for about a week after we got back. It was only meant to be for the rest of that day, but I'd wet my nappy while out playing later that day, so mum said I had to stay in them for the rest of the week to make me learn. I was still self-conscious when outside playing, but after the first day of teasing, everyone just accepted the fact that I was wearing a nappy and ignored it. Some people stared if we were out and about at the park or the shops, but most didn't notice or care. Once I was wearing underpants again, I still went to bed in a nappy until I could keep them dry overnight, and nappy training pants were introduced for daytime, as opposed to full nappies.

Chapter 2 - Age 7 – 9

Before I begin the tale of this era of my life, I'd like to give you a short update from the previous chapter...

I was allowed out of nappies after the week, just as mum had promised. It did feel strange for the first day and I really had to concentrate to make sure I did not have any more accidents, as I didn't want to be put back into nappies during the day again. This went well and I didn't have to wear them in the day after this again. However, if we were going out for the day and there was a risk of no toilets or it was going to be a long trip in the car, mum would give me the nappy trainer pants to put on, as when I needed the toilet, I needed it as soon as possible and sometimes it caused problems. I didn't mind these pants, as they were a thin towel-lined pair of waterproof pants that I wore like underpants and are just for accidents only, so it was for the best that mum gave me these to wear rather than the nappies. However, if you did wet them it was essential you got out of those pants rapid as they were not nice when wet. How I wish we had the pull-ups of today's potty-training regime.

Nighttime, however, was a completely different story. Up until the age of nine, I was in and out of nappies at different stages as the bedwetting continued. Still the terry towelling and plastic pants, of course. I did manage three dry nights, so as was the plan, I was allowed to go nappy free for a bit, then I would have too many accidents in a row, so back into them I went. It was a bit like a roller coaster. The only time I was made to wear them at night without question up to the age of about nine, is when I slept away from home. This had mixed reactions from the households where I was sleeping, but nothing too serious to worry about and at least I slept with the confidence of not having to explain a wet bed! We had moved from Manchester about six months after returning from Blackpool. The relationship with Robert had finished very quickly after Blackpool and mum had met a new man called Andrew, who she later married.

It must have been instant love, as not long after they got together, we moved away. I later found out that my dad was causing problems for my mum and her now-committed boyfriend, so it was decided to move out of the area. We didn't move that far, and we were still able to see our dad and grandparents every other weekend from Saturday morning until Sunday tea time. I of course always had to have a nappy packed in my bag, which mum always reminded me about.

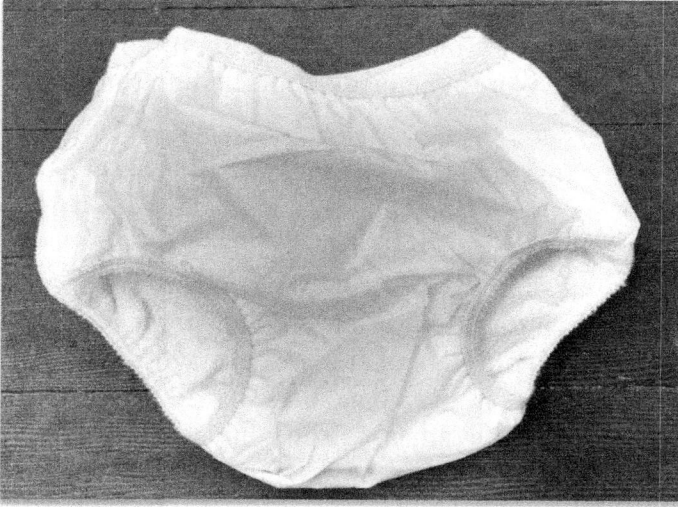

Old fashioned nappy trainer pants!

Mum tried all sorts of ideas to get me dry consistently at night. At about seven years old, the minor punishments started to increase when I wet the bed, which was quite often and did truly wish I could stop. These consisted of, but not limited to, sent to bed earlier, not allowed out after tea, no sweets and so on. Nothing serious, but mum must have thought it might help me learn quicker about not wetting the bed. What they and still some parents these days don't realise. is that kids don't do it on purpose. It's just one of those things. Trust me, we hate waking up in wet beds just as much as parents hate changing and washing the sheets.

One particular day's punishment, and what this book is all about - 'the major events in my life' - was when I had just turned seven and had wet the bed yet again. Normally it would have been a case of either a minor punishment or put back in nappies for a couple of night for bed again if it continued.

But not this time.

On this particular morning, I had wet the bed and after coming down and telling my mum, she huffed and puffed as normal and said, "Okay, Ben. Take your pyjamas off, put them in the bucket and go get your breakfast."

I did as instructed and tucked into my cereal and a small cup of tea. My brothers were also doing the same and were making fun of me as most kids do. I was used to it, but as I got older, the ribbing got a little worse and sometimes it got to me. After breakfast, we were all instructed to go and get our teeth brushed and get ready for school. Alex and I went to one school and Steve to a different one. As we were now in a new bigger house, Alex and I shared a bedroom and Steve had his own, being the oldest. We also had an indoor toilet, which was a luxury for us at first - no cold walks to the loo at night and first thing in the morning. So, Alex and I were in our bedroom getting ready for school when mum walked in carrying a pair of the trainer pants I mentioned earlier.

"Ben, put these on."

"I'm not wearing them," I replied in a kind of cheeky cocky way.

"Oh yes you are!" mum replied sternly. "How many wet beds this week?"

It was only my second, but with only one dry night in between.

"I'm going to school mum, I can't wear them!" I protested.

"Well tough. You are. It's your choice, Ben. Either these or a full nappy - you decide."

She put them on the bed and with one look, made me know in no uncertain terms that if I didn't put them on, there would be trouble and I would end up wearing a nappy to school.

Alex started laughing at me and as I started to get dressed for school I was in a quandary as to what to do. My final thought was 'better these than a nappy', as I was probably going to be put in a nappy for bed anyway now, so I picked them up and went to the bathroom to put them on. I took my underpants off and put on the trainer pants pulling them up and trying to get them as comfy as possible. I then picked up my trousers and put them on, making sure my shirt was tucked in so that there was no way these pants would be visible above the waistband of my school trousers. Now fully dressed, I went back to my bedroom to get my school bag. I then proceeded downstairs.

As I entered the kitchen dining area mum said, "Have you put them on, Ben?"

"Yes, I have. It's not fair!" I protested pointlessly.

She walked over to me and felt my bum to make sure I wasn't lying.

"You will learn Ben. Twice this week."

Alex soon came in and with that my mum said, "Right boys, grab your coats. Let's go."

We left the house and went on the normal route to school, which was about a ten-minute walk or so. As we walked, I could tell I had the training pants on, but thankfully, it didn't make me walk any differently than usual. We got to school and mum kissed us both goodbye and we headed off into class. Throughout the day I was conscious of the fact I had these trainer pants on, so I did things that would not bring attention to the fact and didn't play any rough kind of games that could make my shirt come out of my trouser waist and expose my babyish underwear. The only difficulty came was when I needed the toilet. I had to wait for a cubicle, as I had to pull them down and sit on the loo to have a wee. I can remember sitting there constantly looking up and around making sure no one was spying over the top and ensuring people were making noises when it came to pulling them back up into place. They weren't that rustly, but obviously, they made a different sound to underpants being pulled up. Thankfully, I made it through the day unnoticed and mum was soon at the gates collecting us.

Back home and once we had guzzled down a large glass of orange juice we were told to go and get changed out of our school uniform. This was normally followed by watching cartoons on the TV for a bit and then if the weather was good, we played in the garden. No longer did we have a back yard full of concrete, but we had a proper garden with a lawn, which was so much better to play on. Alex and I started watching TV and Steve went out playing with his mates on his bike. We were living in a council estate area which had only been built two years earlier and was designed for families with young children. There were very few cars about still and playing out was safe, as long as you stayed around the house and didn't wander too far away. Basically, you had to be in shouting distance of the house. That's how we judged how far we could play and as a general rule, it worked!

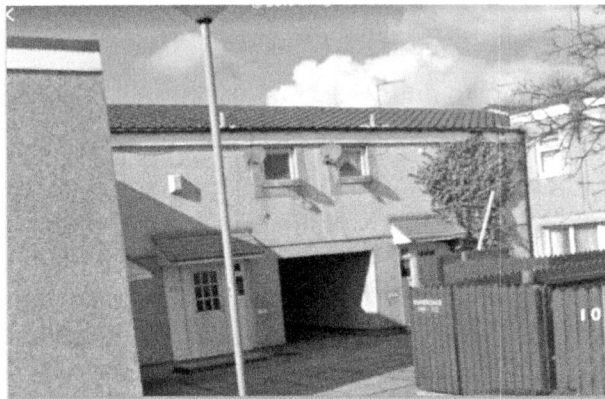

Our first move was to here, a child-friendly place.

As the cartoons finished and the adult programmes started, Alex and I decided to go out in the garden. It was a nice day and quite warm, so we took our toys out, our favourite toys being Action Man, which was really popular for boys our age at the time. As we were walking outside, mum called me back over.

"Ben, come here," she asked.

She gently grabbed my arm and then grabbed at my bum.

"Where are your nappy pants"? She said in a strict questioning manner.

"I took them off when I got back from school. You only said I had to wear them for school."

"No, I did not!" she replied in a stern voice. "Get back upstairs and put them back on now. I will tell you when you can take them off, do you understand?"

I went back upstairs and feeling quite frustrated with this new rule, I put them back on and went back downstairs to go in the garden. Nothing more was said, and I happily played in the garden with Alex until tea was ready. We were all soon called in for tea as Andrew had returned from work, I've no idea what he did at this time, but I also wasn't bothered really. We all sat at the table in the kitchen and ate our tea while talking about our day. Tea finished, and Andrew got his brew and went into the living room to read his paper and chill out.

"Right kids. Come and help clear the table."

We all had a job to do and as soon as we were finished, we were allowed to go back playing until it was time to get ready for bed. We all went outside to the front square outside our house where our friends were now playing and joined in. A bit like in Blackpool a few years earlier, I had forgotten about what I was wearing and just got on with playing. We always had a good time playing outside, always sweating from running about and climbing stuff. We got into trouble quite a lot when returning home for either getting our clothes dirty or annoying a neighbour or something. Nothing serious, but we never learnt, and it was a continuous battle with my mum shouting at us, and us saying sorry until the next time. It was about 7:30 or so when mum called me back in. I thought that my bed wetting punishment was about to end and I could take my trainer pants off.

"Come on upstairs, you! I'd better get you ready for bed."

"It's not bedtime yet!" I replied on the verge of sobbing, as even Alex hadn't been called in yet and it was another hour till bedtime.

"I don't care!" mum replied sternly. "What happened this morning?"

I immediately knew what was coming. As I got into my bedroom, I spotted a nappy laid out on the bed.

"Get undressed Ben and get on the bed".

There was no point arguing, this had happened many times before and no matter how much I pleaded or said I was sorry, or cried, I always ended up wearing the nappy, so I just did as I was told. I sat on the bed and mum told me to lie back. She was still able to lift my bum and slide the nappy underneath me and pin it into place. Next came the plastic pants, putting them on the same way she had always done. With my nappy now on, she told me to put my pyjamas on.

"You will learn, Ben. I'm tired of wet beds. Now go downstairs and play in the garden."

The only saving grace in this horrible situation was that she didn't make me go outside with the rest of the kids. When wearing a full nappy under pyjamas, it was pretty obvious what I was wearing and at my age that would have caused a great deal of teasing.

We all went to bed as normal that night and like clockwork, mum came in the following morning to wake us up to get ready for school. As I got out of bed I prayed I hadn't used my nappy as it didn't feel wet, but before I could double-check, mum came back in and in one swift movement pulled my pyjama bottoms down followed by the plastic pants.

She had a feel of the front and back then said, "Good, it's dry".

The relief was so overwhelming, as I thought if I had wet it, mum would have made me go to school in trainer pants again.

"Looks like yesterday's wearing of nappy pants worked, didn't it?"

I didn't say anything, and she soon told us to hurry up and come down for breakfast. This punishment of trainer pants happened maybe another three or four times over the following few weeks. I was only teased by my brothers, as thankfully you couldn't tell I was wearing them under my trousers. I wore nappies to bed on and off for the following few months until I was able to keep my bed dry on a regular basis. I soon stopped wetting the bed, much to mum's delight, with only the odd accident. Good job really, as I was seven and a half years old now, and way too old for nappies. Things were going really well, then, quite suddenly, we were moving house in a hurry.

The move happened really quickly. No idea why. We didn't even have a last day at school, and then suddenly, one day we are in a removal van heading south with not a clue where we were heading. Turns out it was London. We had moved a long way from Manchester now and that had a big impact on me and my brothers as getting to see our dad and grandparents was now a big issue and made me very, very sad. The area we moved to was just outside of Brixton. The place was a bit rough and it was at the time the Brixton riots were going on. I'm not telling any lies when I say this was a complete culture shock for my brothers and me and my mum. My now-stepdad was from London and I don't think he could wait to get back down there. Turns out he was some kind of relief shop manager or something and looked after various shops while they found new tenants or owners.

This new house was above an off licence and at first, we all hated it. After several weeks, we were really missing our family up north. We hadn't seen my dad or had contact with him and we were told he would not go to court to get access and until he does he couldn't see us. Well, this consequently took nearly five whole years! For five years we never went back up north at all, we just moved from city to city wherever Andrews's job took us. The school was very difficult, as we were in a new one every eight months or so, and as expected, we started rebelling, both at school and at home.

Brixton in the 1980s

Not long after moving south, I started wetting the bed nearly every night again. This made me sad, as Mum had not made me wear a nappy for bed for a while now and I was doing better, so I was pleased. I also hadn't been made to wear any form of protection for trips out for about a year either, so to me, I was doing well and was now like any other eight-year-old. I was pleased with myself, as was my mum! After about three or four weeks of my constant bed wetting, mum had made an appointment at the local doctors, as she thought I could get some help. At least this was the better option, my fear was that I would be punished with wearing nappies again or embarrassed with having one on in the day to make me learn.

On the day of the appointment, we got on a bus and headed into the town centre where on arrival we were greeted by a nice lady who showed us into a room full of charts and various bits of equipment. This man came in and my mum proceeded to tell him the problems. The doctor told her that they had a piece of equipment that they thought would help and with that he instructed the nurse in there with us to bring him some kind of gadget thing. He laid it out on the floor and then placed a sheet over the top of it. Once he had plugged it in, he took a small beaker of water and poured some onto the sheet. As soon as he did it, the box located nearby let out a shrill noise and a white light flashed. It was bloody frightening, I don't mind admitting. The idea was to wake the child as they start to wee so they get up and use the toilet, without wetting the bed as much. This will strengthen the bladder and he will get to know when he needs to get up and use the toilet as his brain will sense the signal of needing to wee. My mum agreed to try it and was given a new one in a box to take home.

Once home, mum put this device onto my bed and located the box underneath my bed. She stated that she hoped this would work. I did too really, as I was getting to the point where I could not go on sleepovers, as I was wetting the bed early every night. Bedtime soon came around and after a cup of tea and a biscuit, Alex and I were sent upstairs to get ready for bed. I put my pyjamas on and climbed into bed and mum came in to kiss us goodnight. She switched the bed alarm on, said goodnight and left the room. Alex and I talked for a while and eventually, we drifted off to sleep.

The next thing I remember was the awful alarm waking me up and a light flashing from underneath my bed. It absolutely terrified me, I started crying and shouting for mum, who came in and turned on the light. She pulled back the covers and noticed a little wet spot on the sheet.

"Go to the toilet, Ben and have a wee."

I did as instructed and on my return, she had put a clean sheet on my bed and I got in. She left the room, again turning the light out as she left. I lay there dreading falling asleep. This alarm truly terrified me. It was so loud and the light made it worse. That was the first night I slept under the covers of my bedsheets. I slept like this for five years or so. I was terrified of sleeping with my head out of the covers, as this nightly routine went on for about four or five weeks. Every night, the same thing happened, and although I supposed it was doing its job, it scared the living daylights out of me every time it went off.

I eventually stopped wetting the bed and we returned the device and life went back to normal at nights with the exception that I would still sleep under the covers for another five years.

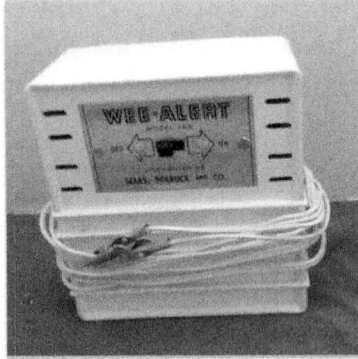

The bedwetting device, the stuff of nightmares!

By the time I was nine years old, we were now living in our fourth or fifth new area. I was getting sick of always being the new kid at school and some schools we went to were really rough, so we had to learn to look after ourselves. We were now living above a supermarket in Essex. We didn't know how long we would be staying, but we were enrolled at the local school and I soon made a friend called Scot. He lived around the corner from me. His parents used our shop most days, so we grew quite close as friends. We would spend days at each other's houses with a parent walking us home after each visit if it was after tea time. One day after school, I was looking for a toy that I hadn't seen since we moved. We always had boxes of stuff that were never unpacked, so I assumed it must be in one of those. I went into the garage at the back of the shop and looked through a couple of boxes and found some stuff that I kept out, even though that wasn't what I was looking for. I kept opening the boxes and was surprised when I found a few old nappies and a couple of pairs of trainer pants that I had worn in the past.

Fear and Joy – a life in and out of nappies

It had been nearly two years now since I had worn a nappy for bed or had to put trainer pants on for going on long trips, but instead of putting them back, for some reason I picked a pair of trainer pants up and opened them up. I've no idea why, but I wondered to myself if they would fit me.

Why would I do this? I've no idea, but the feeling was overwhelming for me to try them on, so I put them in a small box with the other toys I had found and carried it up to my room. As I closed the door to my bedroom I looked in the box again and took out the pants. I still couldn't resist the urge to try them on. This was ironic really, as when I was made to wear them, I resisted and hated them and here I was wanting to try them on.

I checked where everyone was and then I quickly removed my trousers and pulled on the nappy pants. The feeling and emotions I had were extraordinary. As I sat on the bed, they puffed out a bit and then went back to normal. For some strange reason, I really liked how it felt. No idea why, but I did. I stood up and walked around the room, remembering all the times I had been made to wear either these or full nappies in the past.

This time though, it was my choice.

I decided to put them on, and I quite liked the kind of naughty feeling it gave, like I shouldn't be doing it, but I was and nobody knew. I could soon hear voices nearby, so I took them off quickly and hid them in my secret place in my bedroom, put my trousers back on and joined my brothers who were playing downstairs. All that day, I kept remembering what I had just done and how happy I felt and how normal it seemed to me.

Was this a bad thing?

I didn't think so, but I decided that this was my secret and I couldn't let anyone find out what I had done.

A couple of weeks passed by and over that two weeks, I had tried the pants on a few times for a couple of minutes and then put them back in the secret place. I had mixed emotions about what I was doing. I knew it was wrong, but at the same time, it felt nice, not like it had before when I had worn a nappy for its normal purpose in life. These feelings and mixed emotions would stay with me for years until I could find a way to sort these feelings out. Before that could happen though, I would go through other periods in my life where I made wrong decisions or my actions would have a major impact on my life. The last part of this chapter is one of those times, and one that stopped me having any desires for nappies for three or four years.

I had made a really good friend with Scot. His parents and mine were also friends, which meant we could spend time at each other's house. I even did sleep-overs now. We had been living at this particular house for about eight months or so and the weather was getting warmer, as summer was approaching. We played a lot in the woods nearby - making swings and dens out of stuff we found exploring. Scot's family were quite well off compared to us. His house was really nice with a huge back garden and his dad had a really fancy car. On this particular Saturday morning, Scots mum (Sue) had been into the shop to pick up her papers as she did every Saturday and told my mum that they had bought a swimming pool that week and it was now set up. I was welcome to go around if I wanted to and stop for tea.

During breakfast, mum said, "Ben, Scot's mum has invited you round this afternoon to play with Scot and stay for tea. Would you like to go?"

"Yes, can I please mum?"

"Well if you do your jobs before dinner you can go okay?"

I finished my breakfast and got on with my jobs which were sorting the old newspapers out to go back on Monday - a job which I did regularly and got paid a bit of pocket money for. After dinner, I went up to my room and packed my swimming trunks, so I could enjoy Scot's new swimming pool Scot. I couldn't wait!

As I rummaged through my cupboard looking for my goggles, I came across my nappy pants! Being in a really happy, playful mood I suddenly thought I could put these on and try them outside the house.

I quickly picked a pair of shorts out that would cover them. I found a pair of football shorts that were baggy and of suitable size. I packed my trunks, goggles and a towel into my school bag and then, ensuring no one was about, I took my trousers off and put the pants on. As before, it felt really nice and I didn't know why. I pulled my shorts up and put on a long t-shirt and headed downstairs. No one could tell what I was wearing, as my shorts were doing the job well.

With that, I opened the back door and started the short walk to Scot's house. As I walked, I started to remember Blackpool and the other times I had worn either a nappy or these pants and it made me smile. This was my choice and I liked the fact that nobody knew what I was wearing underneath my shorts. On arrival at Scot's, I opened the side gate and went into the back garden. The pool looked great. It was big enough for kids our age to have fun in and it needed a set of ladders that came with it so that we could get in. I couldn't wait.

Scot's mum came out of the house, as did his sister.

"Hi Ben, how are you?" she shouted.

"Great! I like your pool!".

Scot heard me and came running out. "Go and get changed, Ben and play in the pool with me".

Sue then said I could go to Scot's room to get changed. As I walked upstairs' I was so happy, and on entering the room I shut the door so I could get changed. I took off my t-shirt, then my trainers and socks and then pulled my shorts off. I was just stood there with these nappy trainer pants on. I looked at them and was confused as to why I had put them on in the first place. At the same time, I felt happy so I slid them down, folded them up and put them in the bottom of my school bag with my clothes on top so no one could see them. As soon as I got my trunks on, I grabbed my towel and went out into the back yard where we played in the pool for the next two hours. It was amazing.

We both laughed and had so much fun. Scot's sister joined in from time to time, but she just wanted to bathe in the pool whereas

Scot and I were splashing each other and swimming underwater to collect stuff off the bottom. At regular intervals, Sue would bring us some juice and snacks and would usher us out of the pool for a bit. We would sit there in our towels eager to get back in, which, we did most of the day.

The swimming pool that Scot had in his garden.

It was soon tea time and we had to dry off and get dressed for tea.

"Ben, once you've got changed bring your wet stuff down, love and I'll dry it a bit before you go home," Sue shouted to us, as I jumped out of the pool.

"Okay, thanks," and I went upstairs into Scots room to get dressed. I got undressed and dried off properly and then started to get dressed. As I opened my bag I pulled out my clothes, so I could put my trainer pants on first. I opened them up and put them on as I did earlier, got dressed and then went downstairs handing my wet stuff to Sue.

"Tea's ready Ben. Go and sit at the table."

We all had tea and then went into the front room to watch TV for a bit. Scot and I laid on the floor and his mum and dad sat on the settee. Scot then asked if we could go outside in the garden for a bit before I had to go home.

We both went outside and started playing with a football, just kicking it to each other and trying to outdo each other at *keepy ups*. It was a warm night and Sue brought us a drink out. Drink finished, we grabbed the football again and started kicking it to each other. Scot then kicked it a bit too hard and it was going to hit the back-door window, so I reached back to try and grab it and fell over the small wall that led around the back of the house. I landed on my back and as kids do, I let a yell out. Sue came out and saw me lying on the floor trying to get back up.

My elbows were cut, so she told Scot to go inside and get a wet cloth from the kitchen. She asked if I was okay and when Scot returned, she washed the blood off and put a plaster on my elbow.

It was soon time to head off and I said goodbye to his dad, sister and Sue. Scot and I then set off back to my house. I thanked her for a brilliant day and she replied, "You're very welcome, Ben. You can come around anytime, you know that."

We soon reached the shop and as it was still open, we went through the shop door.

"Hi, mum!"

"Hello, love. Have you had a nice day?"

"Brilliant!" I replied.

"I hope you were good. "Do you both want a chocolate bar?"

"Yeeeah!" we both shouted together.

"Ben, take Scot into the back room where we keep the seconds and help yourselves to two items each."

"Thanks, mum."

We both went around the counter and into the back storeroom and selected a choccy bar each and started to eat it straight away.

Once we were finished, we went back into the shop where both mums were still chatting.

"Right Di, we will get off now. Come on Scot... See you tomorrow maybe, Ben?"

"Okay, thank you for having me!"

Scot and his mum then left as a customer came in, so I went out into the back store to get another bar of chocolate. Once she had served the customer, she called for Andrew to come down to look after the shop.

Mum came into the back where I was and said, "Come on Ben, let's get you upstairs and sort your wet kit out. You might need it tomorrow if it's nice weather."

We went upstairs and into my room where I emptied the contents on the floor.

"Do you have anything to tell me, Ben?" mum enquired.

"No mum, why?"

"Are you sure? I had a nice little chat with Scot's mum while you were getting some chocolate."

"I hurt my arm falling over the wall, but it wasn't my fault, honest. Scot kicked the ball too hard, we didn't break anything."

"Right. Take your t-shirt off and let's have a look at this cut."

I did as instructed and removed my top and mum knelt on the floor and removed the plaster. Then it happened!

She yanked my shorts down, revealing my nappy pants. And then in a really strict tone, she demanded, "And what's this all about, then?"

I was in shock. I didn't know what to say at all.

"Well, why have you got them on, Ben. Come on. Answer me! Why are you wearing a bloody nappy?"

I just stood there frozen in place, not knowing what to say. This was the worst thing that could possibly have happened.

"Ben, answer me. Why are you wearing a nappy? Have you not had enough of them already?"

"It's not a nappy," I replied in a really low voice.

"Okay, trainer pants," mum replied.

I was ashamed and embarrassed. I had been found out and it hadn't taken long at all. I was more annoyed that this was my first time wearing one out of the house and I'd been caught. How? I wondered. I'd got out of the house easily enough and back in.

"How dare you embarrass me," she continued. "You don't need them anymore, do you?"

 Mum was really mad, probably quite rightly so, but I just didn't know what to say. I couldn't justify what I was doing nor did I understand why I had done it in the first place. My emotions were all over the place. I didn't know whether to cry or shout out, so I did neither and just stood there feeling sorry for myself and dreading what mum was going to say or do next.

"Where did you get them from?" she asked.

"From the box in the garage."

"Right, well get back down to the garage and bring the box up here now."

I immediately went to the garage. I didn't even ask for my shorts, as I knew what the answer would be. I picked up the box and as instructed, took it back upstairs to my mum. The box had various bits of stuff in it, including some old nappies, clothes and bits and pieces from when we were young. My stomach was churning, as I had a good idea of what was coming. The only thing I couldn't establish in my mind was how bad it was going to be. Punishments for doing anything wrong were getting worse as we got older, normally on the say-so of Andrew, who my mum just agreed with whether she wanted to or not. I could see another Robert coming along month by month.

Fast forward two hours...

I had returned from the garage with the box that mum had asked me to get and mum had now returned upstairs after shutting the shop with Andrew. It was about nine-ish and as it was Saturday night, we were always allowed to stay up a bit longer. Normally, we would be helping in the shop or doing bits around the house if we were not out playing outside. I was still wearing the trainer pants as mum came into my bedroom. Alex and Steve had been downstairs helping Andrew and were now watching TV.

"Well, have you thought of an answer yet, Ben?"

"I don't know," was my reply once again.

I didn't know what to say for the best.

"Get on the bed," mum said in a very stern and demanding voice which frightened me a bit.

She pulled off the trainer pants and then picked up one of the nappies from the box and put it underneath me. Like before, she drew it up between my legs and then pinned it into place. She then grabbed a pair of plastic pants and shook them until they had opened up better, as they had been in the box for quite a bit now. She struggled to get them on, as I was now a bit bigger, but she still managed to pull them all the way up over the terry towelling. The nappy didn't feel as comfortable as I remembered. In particular, the plastic pants felt really stiff and not as soft as they used to be. She then told me to get off the bed at which point, she picked up the trainer pants and told me to put them on. I did as instructed and again - although a little bit tight - I managed to get them on.

"Right, you want to wear trainer pants? Let's see how you like them now!"

I was told to remove my t-shirt and socks and put my other clothes away and then go downstairs into the lounge. I was really worried, I knew I was going to get a good ribbing off my brothers and Andrew, so I tried to do everything as slowly as I could, thereby delaying the impending embarrassment for as long as I could. Not long passed till mum shouted up the stairs.

"Ben, I'm not telling you again. Downstairs now!"

I walked out of my bedroom and down the stairs. The nappy my mum had just put on me, coupled with the trainer pants were very bulky, to say the least, and as this was all I had on, I was scared about what would happen when they saw me. I walked into the front room and straight away my brothers roared out laughing and calling me typical names.

Andrew just said, "Why on earth are you wearing that?"

Mum spoke and told me to sit on the floor where babies should.

"He's been wearing a nappy all day while at Scots' house, Andrew," mum said.

"Why?"

"I've no idea. He won't say, but he doesn't need a nappy, so if he wants to wear trainer pants, then he can wear a proper nappy if that's how he wants to dress".

About half-hour passed and I was really ashamed, sitting there with my brothers still smirking and pointing at me.

Then mum announced, "Right, Ben. Come with me. Babies should be in bed by now! Up the stairs to bed."

I didn't even question it, as this was at least a chance to escape the teasing. I got up and went out of the room as quickly as I could and headed for the toilet.

"Where do you think you're going?" enquired mum. "Upstairs, now!"

"I need a wee before bed, mum!"

"Oh no, you don't. If you want to wear nappies then you can use them! Upstairs now!"

So, off I went to bed in a nappy again, just like old times. As I lay there, I was upset, confused and didn't know what to think. I had done this to myself and my mum was probably right in what she was doing. However, I was still worried about what would happen the next day. Like every night, I soon needed the toilet, but having remembered what mum had said, I just went in my nappy.

It was a strange feeling this time, different than before and whereas before I had hated having a wet nappy on, this time I didn't mind it at all. I was soon back asleep and didn't wake up again until the morning. I didn't even hear Alex come to bed.

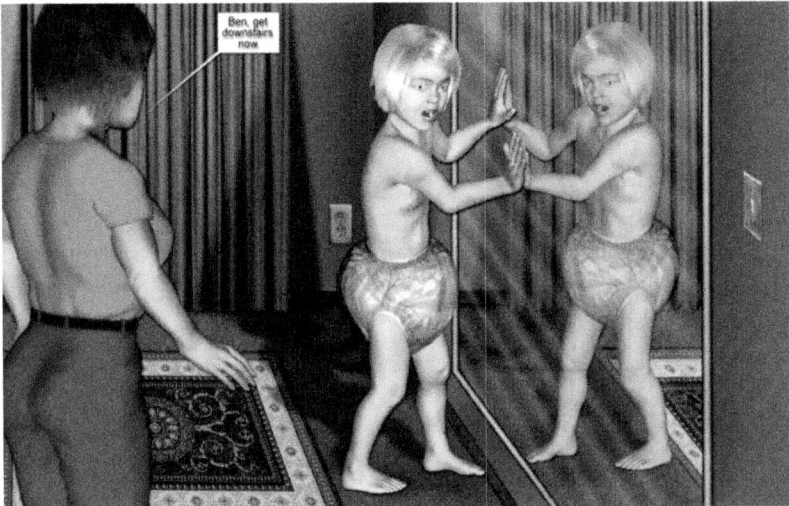

Stalling going downstairs as I had a nappy and trainer pants

on and they were very bulky. I was mortified.

I got out of bed and as I needed a wee and would normally go downstairs to the loo, I remembered last night and just went straight ahead and had a wee as I sat there putting my pyjamas on. Slippers on, I headed downstairs into the kitchen for a drink of milk. My mum and

Andrew were downstairs opening the shop up, so I helped myself to cereal as I normally did. I was about halfway through my breakfast when mum came in. I thought I had better get the first word in and try and get her in a good mood.

"Morning mum, I'm sorry about yesterday."

"Morning love, take your pyjama bottoms off now!"

"I'm sorry mum I won't do it again."

"Ben, don't make me ask again, do it now."

I pulled my pyjama bottoms off and handed them to her and she put them in the laundry bin in the hallway. I finished my breakfast and then took my plates to the sink. As I turned back around mum pulled me into her waist and bent over me and proceeded just like she had done many times before to check my nappy.

"Looks like the baby needs his nappy changed, doesn't he?"

I didn't say anything at all. Just like the day had ended yesterday, it was continuing on.

"Go in the front room and I'll be there in a minute," she said.

As I walked to the front room I thought, "Well it's Sunday today, so back to school tomorrow. I can last the day out with this and let's be honest, I probably deserved it really for wearing the pants in the first place."

I sat on the settee and waited for mum to come in. It wasn't long before she came in carrying a clean nappy, pants and a packet of tissue wipes she had brought up from the shop.

"Right Ben, come on lie on the floor. You know what to do."

I did as she asked and lay down on the floor and mum proceeded to change my nappy.

"Do you like this then, Ben? Is this what you want?"

"No," I replied thinly.

"You must do. Why else would you do what you did?"

"I don't know," I replied.

She was soon pulling up my plastic pants and then telling me to stand up. "No toilet today Ben, do you understand?"

"Yes, mum."

She gave me a t-shirt to put on and my socks and trainers. The absence of any trousers clearly meant I wasn't allowed any for the day. Once I'd finished, she told me to go downstairs into the back of the shop storage area and stay there until she found me something to do. As I walked, I could feel the nappy as it was a bit tighter, since I was bigger now. The pants were a tad small on me, but at least they made the terry nappy less bulky than it could have been, as it was tighter against my body. I went into the storeroom and sat on the chairs drawing on some paper I had found. I was a bit worried about what else was in store for me, but it was school tomorrow and there was no way I could - or would - go to school like this.

Mum came in with a glass of juice for me and said I was staying like this for the day and she didn't want any trouble or moaning at all. I agreed, and she left me to my own devices for a bit. Mid-morning soon came, and mum said I could go back upstairs for a bit to play. I had used my nappy a bit, but not enough to warrant a change - which my mum confirmed following the obligatory nappy check. As I got upstairs, my younger brother saw me and again started laughing and mocking me. Looking back now, I would probably have done the same if it was the other way around, but at the time I was really embarrassed. Steve also did the same once he was up and on his way out to play with his mates.

I went to my room where I had a number of toys to play with and could occupy myself. Alex kept coming in and out and after a couple of hours he stopped taking the mickey and we played a few games and just tried to pass the time. He did say though that I looked stupid and was I going to school like that. I hoped not, and I wouldn't have anyway.

It was soon dinner time and mum had come back up from the shop to make us some dinner as she normally did at weekends. Only Alex and I were in, so at least I wouldn't get any more ribbing, as Alex had exhausted his entire name-calling now. Mum shouted us both down and we sat at the table to eat. As was normal, we both cleared the table and put our pots in the sink ready to be washed.

"Ben, come here." Mum was in the living room and I knew what was coming.

As I walked in, she was reading a magazine and drinking a brew. "Right, go to the bathroom. You can take your own nappy off, wash yourself and then come back here".

Great I thought.

So off I ran to the bathroom and did as ordered. My nappy was a bit wet now, as I'd had it on since I got up. I put it in the bath and then returned to the front room where mum was waiting.

She just glanced up from her magazine and said, "Well, on the floor then!" At the side of her, was a clean nappy ready for me. "You wee in it. You take it off and clean yourself, Ben".

I was then unexpectedly put back in a nappy and then told I could go outside and play.

Before she went downstairs, she came up to my bedroom and said, "Ben, rinse that wet nappy out in the bath and then put it in the washing machine."

"Okay," I replied in a sullen voice. I really had thought I had been punished enough.

Obviously not!

About mid-afternoon, I was called down to do some jobs in the shop. As I went back into the storeroom, mum came in with a pair of shorts.

"Here, put these on," and handed me back the shorts I had worn yesterday. I can tell you something, it was good to get my shorts back on, and even if I was wearing a nappy, at least it was hidden. "Right, go and see what shelves need filling, then do what you can, okay?"

"Yes, mum."

I went out into the shop and started to see what shelves needed doing and made a list, so I didn't have to remember them all. I started getting stuff from the back and filling up the shelves and I tried to do it as quickly and as neatly as I could, so I could get back into mum's good books. It felt weird having a nappy on with people coming into the shop and seeing me, yet not knowing.

Thankfully, it didn't show much like it did when I was younger. Being bigger meant the nappy was smaller on me, so that was a good thing. I continued to use it, as mum had said I still wasn't allowed to use the toilet, so towards the end of the afternoon, it was getting a bit wet. Just before tea, Steve came back in and as I had my shorts on, either forgot what I was wearing or just didn't bother. Anyway, he just went upstairs and I carried on in the shop helping mum and Andrew. Mum then called me into the shop, so I thought it was to get more stuff or something. As I entered, Scot and his mum were there.

"Hiya Ben!" Scot exclaimed. "Hiya," I replied.

Mum and Sue started talking, while we went into the back to get some chocolate. "Did you get a telling off last night, Ben?" Scot then asked.

"Why, how do you know?"

"Mum told me on the way back that she thought you were having problems, so asked your mum when we dropped you off."

"What problems? I'm alright!"

"No," Scot butted in. "My mum saw your nappy when you were round at our place yesterday, so wanted to know if you were okay as she hadn't been told."

Fear and Joy – a life in and out of nappies ▐

Now the penny dropped! I thought I had managed to conceal what I was wearing yesterday, but obviously not good enough. I later found out how this had come about. Maybe a month later when I was round at Scot's house, Sue told me that when she dropped me back at home that she had noticed I was wearing a nappy and had asked my mum why and quite innocently if I needed to wear something if I was going in their swimming pool again.

This had embarrassed my mum and once she had explained to her that she had no idea what I was doing wearing one, they had both laughed apparently. She told Scot's mum what she was planning and not to invite me round the following day.

Scot asked if I was wearing a nappy and I just said, "Yes, mum's making me wear one today."

Scot laughed and said, "No way!" and tried to see if he could see it, which he couldn't. "Are you going to school in one tomorrow?"

"No way," came my very definite reply.

We were both then called into the shop, as Scot's mum was leaving, so they both said goodbye and left. I went back to what I was doing and mum went upstairs to prepare tea for us.

It was soon time for tea and we were all called to sit at the table. I went up and sat in my usual place.

Steve then said, "You still got a nappy on then?"

"Yeah, why?"

He just laughed and then carried on eating. Once we had finished, the table was cleared and mum then told me to do as before and take my nappy off and go to the front room.

I must have been taking a while as the shout soon came, "Ben, hurry up will you please?"

I made my way to the front room whereas before I was put in a nappy, but not allowed to put my shorts on. There I was again, wandering around the house in just my nappy and a t-shirt. I went up to my room and just tried to entertain myself until bedtime. As bedtime drew near, Alex and I were called down to have our evening drink and supper. Mum asked us if we had gotten our school bags ready and we were then given a cup of milk and a biscuit and told to go in the front room. Andrew just looked at me and shook his head as I passed him and sat on the floor.

Once we had finished our drinks, mum then said "Right, come on you two. Bedtime".

We said goodnight to Andrew and went upstairs. Alex went to the bathroom and mum followed me up.

"Up on the bed, Ben. Hurry up, I've got a programme to watch."

Whereas before I had to take my own nappy off and so on, time was important tonight, so in no time at all Mum was taking off my nappy, cleaning up and fastening me back into a nappy ready for bed.

"Night, night," she said, as she walked out of the room switching the light off.

Another day ended as it has started, but there was hope tomorrow that I would get my underwear back. The same thing happened that night. I woke up needing a wee, but I had no choice as I would not be able to hold it till morning, so I just let go and had a wee in my nappy. Morning came quickly, and mum was shouting through the door for us to get up. We all got up and went downstairs for breakfast and then mum told us to go and get washed and ready for school.

"Ben, take your nappy off in the bathroom, leave it in the bath and go and get ready."

"I don't have to wear one to school, do I mum?"

"No, and count yourself lucky, young man, now go and get ready."

I raced out of the kitchen, took my nappy off and cleaned as best I could, then ran upstairs to put my underpants back on. Relief, I really did think she was going to send me to school in a nappy or the trainer pants, but I was given a lifeline.

We went to school as normal, mum walking Alex and me to the gate where I met up with Scot and Alex's friends. We said goodbye to our mums and then went into the playground. Scot immediately asked if was wearing a nappy to which I replied, 'absolutely not' and that the punishment was over.

"Can't believe you had to that, Ben."

"I know, good job mum was in a good mood this morning."

"Did you have to wee or anything in it?"

"No way," I said, lying to cover up my embarrassment.

"I could use the toilet when I wanted to," and with that, we started to join in playing with a football and I soon forgot about the weekend's activities!

The last bell soon went, and we ran out of the school doors towards the gates where we would be met by our mums. Scot and I always left together and as usual, our mums were there. Alex soon joined us, and we started walking home. My older brother walked himself home, so Scot, Alex and I played on the way home while the mums chatted about stuff. We were soon at Scot's road and as the mums were chatting, his mum invited me round after tea if I wanted.

"I'll bring him home a half-hour before bedtime, Di."

Scot and I looked at each other and gave the thumbs-up signal to say 'cool' and so on. We then headed back home and went up to our bedrooms to get changed and then do our jobs in the shop. I got a glass of pop as we all normally did once home from school and a couple of biscuits to tide us over till tea time. I ran upstairs and put my school uniform away and unpacked my school bag. Alex then came in and said mum wanted me downstairs.

I went downstairs, and sure enough mum called me into the front room. "Lie down please, Ben."

"What? No mum, please don't put me in one again."

"Ben, lie down now. I let you take it off for school, didn't I? Well, you're not at school anymore, so lie down."

I started crying as I thought this punishment was over. I lay down on the floor still crying while mum removed my shorts and underpants and pulled my t-shirt up, so she could put my nappy back on.

"Look, Ben," she said in a kind of childish way. As I looked at what she was holding it was a bigger terry-towelling type nappy. "This should fit you better."

She folded it up a bit and then lifted my legs and slid the towelling underneath me. She then grabbed the two opened nappy pins from the floor, put one in her mouth as she always did and then proceeded to bring the towel up through my legs and pin it into place.

She then grabbed an unopened packet of plastic pants and said, "These are for bigger boys just like you".

She showed the picture on the packet and sure enough, it was a pair of plastic pants for ages 5-7. I didn't even know they made them that big!

She unfolded them and shook them so that she could see which way round to put them on and then just like the thousand times before, scrunched them up and told me to lift my legs so she could slide them over my feet and up to my knees. She then lifted one leg and tugged on the pants to get one side over my nappy then the other.

"Right stand up." I got up and she pulled up the pants to cover the nappy completely. "There you go, baby."

She picked up my shorts and took them with her leaving me exactly as I had been yesterday - in just a t-shirt and nappy. As I stood up to walk back up to my bedroom, I got the same feeling I had when I was younger as the bulk was a lot thicker now that she had put an older kid's size nappy on me. I don't know to this day where she got them from as I never dared asked. Suffice to say, they fit me properly, much better than the other ones I had been wearing. The pants had enough room as they were not as tight and puffed up if I sat down or put any type of trousers or shorts on. The larger nappy made it easier for mum, as she didn't have to struggle to put me in smaller nappies and pants.

I was mortified, to be honest.

I went upstairs where Alex was playing in the room and he looked at me and asked, "What you back in nappies for Ben?"

"Mum said I have to."

"That nappy looks big on you."

"I know," I said softly.

"You look funny," he said and started laughing.

I glanced at myself in the mirror on my cupboard door. I did, I looked stupid wearing a t-shirt and this massive nappy. I felt ashamed and I wished I'd never found the trainer pants now as this wouldn't have been happening. I was hating wearing these things and being made to wee in them. I was being treated like a baby, not in all ways, but it was bad enough. But I thought to myself, well, it's my fault isn't it, I wore the pants to start with, so I only have myself to blame. It didn't make me feel any better though and I started to think how long this would go on for, hoping it was maybe just another couple of days. Surely mum would get fed up of putting nappies on me and having to wash them.

Both Alex and I went down to do our jobs in the shop. I stayed in the back as I had no shorts on, so found bits to do there. Steve soon returned home from school. He had been playing nearby with a few of his mates. He came into the storeroom where I was and really took the mickey out of me. I was so embarrassed I could have cried.

"Steve, leave him alone please, go upstairs and get changed," mum interrupted. Saved… not that it made any difference. I was still spending the night like this.

We were all soon sat having tea, Andrew watching the shop, so mum could sit with us. Steve said to mum that I looked funny dressed as I was.

"Of course, he does. It's Bens fault though, that's what he wants to wear, so he can wear them properly, isn't that right, Baby Ben?"

I didn't say anything, as I was too busy eating and too embarrassed to join in this conversation.

"You should make him play outside with one on mum. All our friends would see him in them and should teach him not to wear a nappy."

He laughed as he said it and Alex joined in.

"I'll decide what's happening, not you two, now clear the table and Steve can you wash the pots tonight, so I can go back in the shop please, and Alex, you dry."

"What about me?" I asked.

"You are going to Scot's house, remember?"

"Oh yeah, well can I go and get changed please?"

"Into what?" she asked.

"My underpants and trousers please mum?"

"You have a choice tonight, Ben. Now go upstairs to your room and I'll be up shortly."

I waited in my room, trying to work out what the choice would be. I just prayed I could take my nappy off. Mum came in and soon explained the choice I had.

"I spoke to Scot's mum about tonight, so you can either go in a clean nappy, use the toilet and keep it dry so that you're ready for bed when you come home or, you can wear your trainer pants again take a nappy with you and put it on before you come home, so I don't have to get you ready."

"Can I not just wear my underpants please mum? I'll put my nappy straight back on when I come home?"

"Ben, I just gave you your choices. You wanted to wear nappies to Scot's house, didn't you? So now you have a choice of nappy, don't you?"

"I don't want to go, mum. I'll stay here."

"You are going to Scot's, it's as simple as that. How many more times do I have to tell you, Ben? You really embarrassed me on Saturday, so hurry up and make up your mind or I'll decide for you."

I was mortified. Either choice had its major downsides and I couldn't decide which was the least embarrassing.

"Ben, you've got one minute to decide. By the time I get back, you had better have made up your mind or I will make it for you."

She left the room and a million thoughts and what-ifs went racing through my mind. What do I do? Scot knew what was happening and that I had worn a nappy because of Sunday, but I was in the safety of my own house and easily brushed it off. You couldn't really tell what I had on as my shorts did the job of hiding them pretty well.

Mum came back in "Well, what's it to be?"

I decided that as I wouldn't be able to put a nappy on myself, as I had never done it before, it was best to do the 'nappy on, but not use it' option. So that was it then.

I laid on the bed while mum changed me into a clean nappy and then gave me some shorts to put on. I then picked out the longest t-shirt I could find and put that on, which did half a job of hiding it.

"Right Ben, use the toilet and keep that dry for bed tonight, okay?"

"Yeah," I replied, not really looking forward to going to Scot's now.

"See you later then. Have a nice time."

And with that, she ushered me out of the door.

I set off on the short walk to Scot's, really conscious of what I was wearing and wondering if there was any way I could get out of it. But being only nine years old, my young cunning brain wasn't good enough to think of something that quick. I soon arrived at Scot's and went through the side gate as I normally did.

Scot was in the garden playing football and shouted, "Hi Ben, It's footy time!"

I walked up the path to him and he noticed my face and mood pretty quickly, as I was normally happy to be at Scot's house.

"What's up?" Scot asked.

I thought the best way was to get this over and done with.

"Mum's still making me wear a nappy."

"Really, have you got one on now?"

"Yeah." Scot laughed a bit and then said, "Sorry Ben, I didn't mean to laugh. I just can't believe your mum made you put a nappy on. That's cruel."

I didn't answer at first and then I just said, "Please don't tell anyone at school."

"I won't Ben, not your fault is it?" Scot replied. "Did you put it on yourself?"

"Of course! No way I was allowing mum to do me like a baby."

"Don't worry, only I know".

I realised I now had a good friend in Scot. I had only lived here a short while, but we had really bonded and did everything together and had I stayed in the area we would have remained friends for life and become my best mate and so on.

Sue then came out and said, "Sorry Ben, it's my fault. I told your mum."

"It's okay, you didn't know," I replied.

She had always been nice to me and even at my age, I couldn't blame her. She thought she was doing the right thing.

"Scot, go inside for ten minutes and make some drinks while I talk to Ben."

"Okay mum," and with that Scot left us.

"Come and sit down Ben, I know what your mum is making you wear tonight. She asked me to make sure you still had it on when you got here. I understand what she is trying to do and I know it's hard for you love, but I have to go along with your mum's wishes, okay?"

"Yeah, thanks it's okay. I'm alright. Scot said he won't tell anyone."

"I know he won't, he likes you, Ben. He's not had many friends since he started school here."

"Can I go and play with Scot now?"

"Yeah, of course. Ben, if you want to take your nappy off while you're here, you can okay? Just put it back on before you go home."

"Can I?"

"Course you can. I'll keep it a secret if you will!"

"Thank you," I replied in a happy and relieved voice.

"Go up to Scot's room and take it off there, leave it behind the door and then you can go and play okay?"

I raced up to Scot's room and shut the door. What a relief to take it off for a bit. I pulled off my shorts and plastic pants in one motion and then unpinned the nappy and threw it behind the door. What a relief it was to get that off! Scot's sister would be around later, and I didn't want her knowing or seeing that I had to wear nappies.

Scot and I had a really good time playing in the garden and then sitting around drinking juice and when needed, I could use the loo. I felt so much better and even Sue had been good about it and thought of a way to help me. I know she said she understood what mum was doing, but I think she felt sorry for me in a way. To her way of thinking, she was the reason I ended up like this, although I instigated it, so I assumed she was trying to make up for it in some way. I didn't blame her in any way then and even if I were to meet her now, I wouldn't. She was kind to me and understood, as did Scot, even though he was only nine like me.

It was nearing time for me to go home and Sue came into the garden and said, "Ben you're going to have to get ready in about five minutes."

Ay,

Scot then asked, "Have you got to put a nappy back on?"

"Yeah I have to, or mum will shout at me. You promise you won't tell anyone, Scot?"

"Course I won't, Ben. I promise."

We played for another few minutes and then Scot said that I'd better go and get ready for the walk home to my house. I went inside and up to Scots room. As I entered the room the nappy that I had put behind the door was now folded on the bed with the plastic pants on top ready for me to put on.

I thought to myself, "How am I going to do this? Mum has always done it."

Anyway, I put it on the floor as it was folded and then grabbed the two pins and opened them up. I pulled the towel between my legs and kept adjusting it till it fit like it normally does. I grabbed one of the pins and managed to stick it in, then the other and then pulled on the plastic pants. I was quite chuffed with myself. I'd done it, my first nappy! As I got up, I realised it wasn't quite tight enough and would have eventually fallen down. It didn't feel as comfy either, so I shouted to Sue who was waiting downstairs.

"You okay, Ben?" she asked.

I started crying a bit and asked Sue, "Can you help me, please? I can't do it right."

She came straight up the stairs and I told her what I had done, but that it wasn't quite right.

"Ben, don't cry love. it's okay, come on."

We went into Scot's room and she closed the door. "What's wrong, love?"

"It won't stay up when I'm walking, and I can't do it and my mum will shout at me," I replied, still crying.

Sue then replied in a really caring soft voice, "Come on Ben. Don't cry. I'll sort it out."

She then asked me to pull my shorts down, so she could try and sort it out for me.

"It's a long time since I've done a nappy, Ben. Let's have a look."

She didn't make a fuss or anything or make me lie down on the floor, which was a relief. She just pulled my plastic pants down just enough, so she could see the pins. She unfastened them one at a time and then put them back in, so she got the nappy a bit tighter and in the right place.

"How's that Ben? Is that okay?"

"Yes, thank you," I replied, truly thankful.

She then pulled up the dreaded plastic pants and made sure the nappy was all tucked in.

"There you go, all done!"

"Thank you, Sue. I'm sorry," I replied.

"Don't be sorry love, how would you know how to do it yourself. I only just remembered how to do it myself!" she laughed.

"Scot wore disposable nappies when he was a baby. I haven't done these since his sister was a baby. Come on then, get your shorts on and I'll take you home."

We were soon heading up the road towards the shop, chatting away with each other and just having fun. Sue never made a fuss or asked me any more questions about it. She probably thought it was bad enough as it was. To me though, I was happier than when I had left the house to come here. Just by someone showing me kindness and understanding made all the difference, and Scot being a good mate made me feel normal. Also, the fact that they both didn't embarrass me and tried their best to keep my dignity, which even to this day I appreciated.

We soon arrived home and I went into the shop and said hello to my mum.

"Thank you for bringing me home. See you tomorrow Scot!"

My mum then spoke and thanked Scot and Sue for having me and asked if all was okay.

"All fine Di, no problem, see you at school tomorrow, Ben."

As they left, mum looked at me and asked, "Is your nappy dry?"

"Yes," I replied. "I've used the toilet."

"Good. Go and get your pyjamas on and I'll be up shortly."

I raced upstairs and into my room where I quickly got changed and went downstairs to watch TV in the front room. Steve and Alex were there who, as normal stated the obvious about my attire. I just ignored them and sat down and watched TV till mum came up. Once we had had our milk, Alex and I went to bed and Steve was allowed to stay up longer.

The following morning went as the previous day had done in that I could take off my nappy and put my normal underwear back on for school. On return from school, I was put back into nappies and this went on for the whole week with the odd tease from my brothers and mum asking me if I still liked wearing nappies, to which I always said no.

I'd gotten used to it by Friday tea time, but I still hated the fact that every night after school I was put back into nappies until the following morning. By Wednesday I was taking them off myself still and washing them by hand, ready to put them in the washing machine. Once finished, I had to take them out and put them on the side ready for mum to sort out. I must have washed a hundred nappies by the weekend and I suppose I knew how mum felt when I was younger. Another embarrassing bit as the week wore on, was coming home from school and seeing about four nappies and as many plastic pants hung on the washing line. It was like the old days in Manchester.

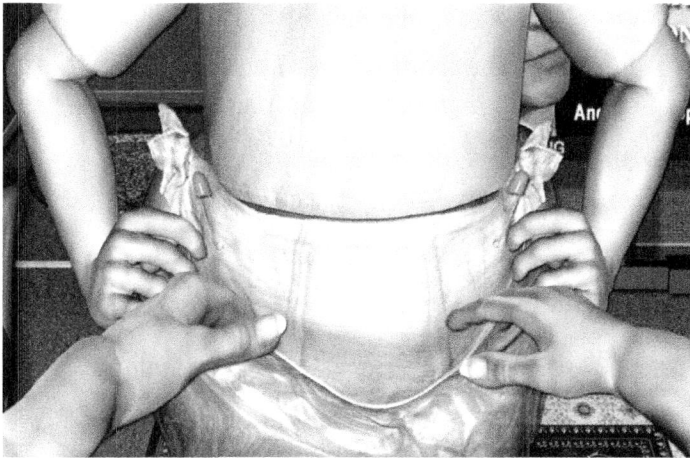

Sue helping me re-fasten the pins so my nappy stayed up!

Saturday morning started out as normal with the exception that after breakfast, I was told to go and take my nappy off, wash and then go to the living room. As there was no school I was obviously having a nappy put back on. I went into the front room where mum was waiting.

"Lie down, no school today."

I did as she asked, and a clean nappy went back on.

"Mum, when can I stop wearing these, I won't do it again?"

"When I say you can," she replied firmly.

I could tell Mum was in a rush. She was going out shopping with her friend who owned the hairdressers on the shop row we lived on. Mum really forced my nappy on, a bit rough really, but it was soon done. Nappy now on, but no shorts, I was told I could go back to my room.

As I walked into the bedroom, Alex didn't say anything. I expect he was used to seeing me dressed like this. We just got on and played until mum came back about dinner time. I'd had to use my nappy, so I went and asked mum if I could take it off as it was uncomfortable.

"No," came the terse reply, "I'll sort you out in a minute."

I went back into the front room to wait and watched TV. Mum soon came in carrying a clean nappy and pants.

"I'll go and take this off and wash mum," I said.

"Don't bother. Just lie down on the floor."

I laid down and mum did the full job, cleaning me up and then putting on a new nappy.

As she was putting on my plastic pants she asked, "Are you going to Scot's today?"

"I don't know if he's in," I replied.

"Well, go around and see. It's not that far."

"Can I put my shorts on though?" I asked, half in fear of the answer.

"Yes, of course, you can if you're going out."

It was just so weird. I was having a normal conversation that a ten-year-old would have with his mum, but I was getting my nappy changed at the same time. I wasn't sure if my mum was coming around to the idea that I'd learnt my lesson, but I was hoping it would end soon. Although, if I'm being honest, I was getting used to it by now and as long as I had shorts or trousers on, it started to become normal.

Andrew came up shortly after I'd had my nappy changed and said that Scot's dad had been in on his way out to pick up some bits for his journey and said I could go around today if I wanted to. Brilliant, I thought. I loved going to Scot's to play.

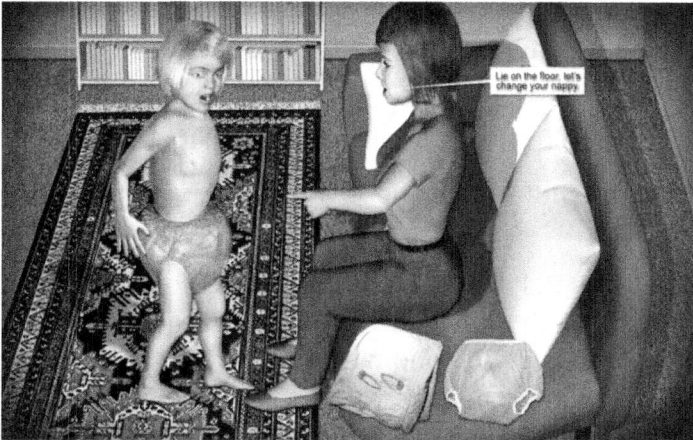

How it was over the week for every nappy change!

Scot knew that I would have a nappy on, and so would his mum, so I wasn't worried. I was still a bit embarrassed about it, but not that concerned. I packed my swimming trunks and mum brought in a clean nappy and pants, in case I needed it.

"I'll use the toilet at Scot's, mum," I said. "I don't have to wee in my nappy, do I?"

"No, okay," and she took it back out of my room.

Relief.

Once I was packed, I said goodbye to mum and headed out, saying bye to Andrew who was in the shop where he always was. I ran - well I tried to run - around to Scot's and on arrival, I was greeted like I always was.

"Hiya, Ben!" Scot shouted. He was already in the pool. Sue came out and repeated the welcome.

"Hiya, can I go in the pool, please?"

"Of course, you can, love".

I went into the house as Scot was telling me to hurry up.

As I went through the kitchen Sue asked me, "Are you wearing a nappy again, love?"

"Yeah," I replied, without a hint of embarrassment.

"Okay, just put it on the floor when you take it off, ready for going home later."

And with that, I did the same as the previous Saturday and was soon enjoying the swimming pool with Scot. Sue came out to sit in the garden and Scot's sister and dad were away until the next day. Scot had told me that his gran wasn't well, so they had gone down to London to help his granddad. I think Sue was grateful for the distraction of us two running riot in the garden.

The day went by, having lots of fun. We had a chippy dinner which was a real treat for me and then in between jumping in the pool, we played football and lots of other games, some of which Sue joined in. It was nearing tea time and mum had said I had to be back before tea. Sue asked if I wanted to stay for tea, but I couldn't say yes or no, as I'd have to ask my mum.

"I can get dressed and go and ask, as it's nearly tea-time anyway," I offered.

"I'll be quicker on my own, Ben. I'll go and ask, you stay here with Scot and I'll ask Joyce to watch you till I get back".

"Okay," we both shouted and carried on dunking each other in the pool.

Sue leaned over the fence and shouted to Joyce, her next-door neighbour and explained the situation and Joyce came around to watch us, while Sue went back to my house. Thankfully, Mum agreed I could stay for tea, but asked Sue to have me home by seven pm, as we were going out. I had my tea at Scot's and then after another couple of hours, it was time to get dressed to go home. What a fabulous day it had been.

Scot and I were worn out. We had laughed and played all day long, Sue commenting that she didn't know where we got our energy from several times. I went upstairs and into Scot's room where I found my clothes and nappy laid out on the bed just like last week. I tried the same method to put my nappy back on but again couldn't get it as tight enough so that it stayed up around my waist, even with the plastic pants.

I called for Sue, who as she came towards the door said, "Do you need a hand again Ben? You should have asked me before you came upstairs, instead of struggling with your nappy."

"I didn't want to Sue, coz it's embarrassing."

"I know it is, but there is no need to be embarrassed at all. I did it last week didn't I and we had no problems, did we?" I just nodded my head in agreement.

"Well come on then, let's get it on properly and get you home."

As before, she just pulled down my plastic pants enough to get to the pins and put them in properly so that my nappy stayed up and did all she could not to embarrass me.

We left the house and headed up the road, Scot and I talking away and jabbering at Sue who was laughing at us.

As we entered the shop, Andrew greeted us, as mum was upstairs getting ready to go out.

"Howdy Ben. Mum's upstairs with B."

B was our babysitter. She was a friend of one of the staff members that worked part-time in the shop. I never got to know her real name. We just called her B, and I think she was either French or Italian. Nice lady though.

"I thought we were going out, Andrew?" I asked quizzically.

"No Ben. Just me and mum tonight. B is here to look after you all."

Sue then stepped in and asked Andrew if I could have a sleepover at her house.

"I don't see why not, but ask Di, as she's made the arrangements."

My mum came down shortly after. I took no time to ask...

"Can I stay at Scot's tonight, please mum?"

"Sorry Di, it was my idea," explained Sue. "I thought you were all going out."

"Please mum, I've been good haven't I, Sue?" I begged.

"I'm not sure Ben," mum replied.

"Please mum!" I begged again. "I'll be good and back in the morning to help out in the shop!"

"Sue, can I have a word?" Mum interrupted, and I guessed what they were going to talk about - my nappies. "Wait there, Ben".

Mum and Sue went into the back for a few minutes then came back out.

"Okay, Ben," mum announced. "You can go to Scot's tonight, but there is no change to your routine, so if Sue is okay with that then yes, you can go. Is that understood?"

Scot and I ran upstairs like a dog after a bone, giggling and joking as we knew we were in for a fun night. I picked up my school bag and put my pyjamas in and some toys and then went down to the kitchen. Mum and Sue had come up and Sue asked Scot to go downstairs to the shop and get some chocolate as a treat. My mum then handed me a carrier bag with a couple of nappies in it and plastic pants.

"Ben, Sue will make sure you're ready for bed okay, no arguments. Just because you're sleeping away from home doesn't mean the punishment stops, does it?"

"No mum", I answered. But no amount of punishment could lower my excitement for the night to come.

"Sue knows what your routine is and maybe tomorrow we can have a talk. You wear your nappy to bed, no arguing, and if Sue tells me any different, there will be trouble."

"Okay, mum," I promised.

Mum then spoke to Sue. "Are you sure you don't mind Sue? I'd leave him out nappies, but he's been in one for over a week now and he might -"

Sue interrupted, "It's fine Di, honestly. He's been wearing his nappy all day today, so it won't matter overnight. He will be fine. He's no trouble, honestly."

Mum then gave me a kiss and a hug and told me she would be around tomorrow to pick me up, when it was time to come home.

We all headed back to Scot's and we were both in such a good mood that Sue had to tell us to calm down more than a few times. I'd forgotten that I was wearing a nappy and as soon as we got in, we just started playing in the front room while Sue put a camp bed into Scot's room for me. I was going to sleep in his sister's bed, but we both agreed we wanted to stay in the same room. What a laugh we were having!

We were soon in the garden again when I needed the loo. I just went in my nappy, I know I shouldn't have, but I just did. I don't know if it was a habit or because I wanted to, but for the rest of the evening, I just weed in my nappy as I did at home. Sue let us carry on playing till way past my normal bedtime. It was almost 9:30 when our play was interrupted.

"Scot, go and get your pyjamas on, please?"

"Okay mum, you coming up Ben?"

"Yeah, I'll come up too -"

"Ben, you stay here a minute please," Sue interrupted.

Scot went upstairs and then Sue said, "I know you've been wearing a nappy for bed every night, so you will have to put one on tonight, just in case, as your mum thinks you might wet the bed if we leave your nappy off."

I didn't even question her. I just said. "Yeah, okay, mum said I'd have to wear one."

"We can go to Sophie's room for this. There's not much room in Scot's, as I've put the camp bed up."

For some reason, I wasn't bothered at all. Maybe it was because she had been so nice to me the last two times, she had helped me that I knew she wouldn't embarrass me or anything like that. We went upstairs into Sophie's room. She opened up my bag and pulled out my pyjamas and a clean nappy and pants.

"Right, Ben. How does your mum normally get you changed?"

"On the bed," I said. "It's how my mum has always done it."

"Okay, take your clothes off and lie on the bed for me."

I got on the bed and I didn't even care that my wet nappy was now on full view. I should have been, but I wasn't. Sue then smiled and started laughing.

"Have you had an accident. Ben, or did you forget that you could use the toilet?"

"I did a wee coz I didn't want to stop playing to use the toilet," I replied, laughing.

Laughing along with me, she said, "You cheeky monkey, it's a long time since I've changed a wet nappy so here goes!"

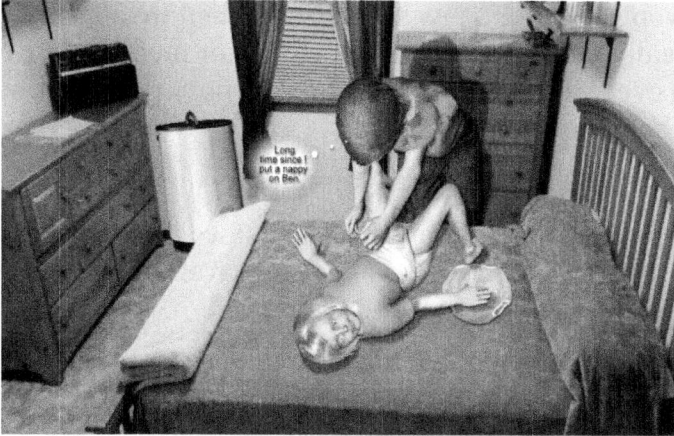

Sue putting my night nappy on. She was wonderful and I

really liked her.

She pulled off my plastic pants and unpinned my nappy, removing it and placing it on a towel at the side of me. She did a quick wipe and then reached for the clean nappy. She placed it under me, after asking me to lift my bum. I thought to myself how my mum normally did this for me. Having finally got it into position and fitting right, she pinned it into place and then adjusted it, making sure it was comfy for me. Then she grabbed the plastic pants and asked me to lift my legs so she could ease them over my feet, trying her hardest to wriggle them up my legs.

As I got off the bed, she tucked any bits of towelling that was poking out of the plastic pants and then said, "There you go, Ben. All done!"

It was wrong to think about it, but I felt *great*. I really did. Sue had got me ready for bed without any fuss, laughing with me and understanding why I needed or had the nappy on in the first place. Sue was like Jane was in Blackpool those years before.

Scot then walked in. "Wow, that's a massive nappy, Ben!"

"Don't be cruel, Scot," Sue replied, without any venom.

It went silent for a few seconds and then we all started laughing really hard. This was so much fun for me. I was wearing a nappy and everyone was laughing *with me,* not *at me.* That had never happened before ever.

"Right boys, if your good, you can stay up a bit longer."

We both were so happy and asked if we could go downstairs and watch some TV. As we were about to leave, Sue shouted out, laughing, "Ben, don't forget your pyjamas!"

I put my pyjama top on but did not bother with the bottoms. Why? I don't know, I just felt comfortable, I suppose.

I was about to run downstairs to join Scot when Sue said, "Ben, are you not putting your bottoms on?"

"Do I have to?" I replied.

"Course not, if you don't want too. Look love, I know why you're having to wear nappies. Your mum told me and it's nothing to be ashamed of. It's not wrong. Everyone has their own ways, you know."

"Mum thinks it's wrong though, that's why I'm wearing nappies again."

"She doesn't think they are wrong, love. It is just her way of making you stop. Do you want to stop wearing them, Ben?"

"I don't know. I just wanted to try one on again."

"It's okay, Ben. I understand. Look, Scot and I know you're wearing one, don't we? So, if you want to just wear a nappy and see what it's like, you can. No one will judge you here".

She left the room and I just stood there thinking about what Sue had just said. I don't think I understood really, but in a way, I was hoping she was saying it was okay for me to just wear a nappy tonight.

I pondered her words for a bit longer - a nine-year-old with a thousand thoughts going through my mind. I stood there in a pyjama top and a nappy, holding my pyjama bottoms. Scot knew I had a nappy on. He'd just walked in on me having it put on by his mum, and Sue had put me in the nappy I was wearing, so it really must be okay.

Only a minute had passed when Sue shouted up, "Are you coming down, Ben? I've made some hot milk for you both!"

In that split second, I threw my pyjama bottoms on the floor and went downstairs wearing just a nappy and my top. I walked into the front room where Scot was sat on the floor, having gotten a game out.

"That's a big nappy, Ben," Scot exclaimed, with no malice whatsoever.

Sue walked in with our milk and put it on the table. She turned around and saw me stood there with an obvious nappy and just smiled. I sat on the floor with Scot and started to play snakes and ladders with him while Sue watched TV. Wow, this was such a great feeling to me.

Ever since I found the trainer pants, this was all I wanted. To have fun and be accepted for who I was.

I suppose that in a way, it was wrong for me to be wearing nappies, but at the same time, I was happy. No one bothered me, and Scot and Sue accepted who I was. Even at the age of ten, this had a profound impact on me in later life. I knew that if I found a genuine honest person with an open mind and no matter what or who you were, it didn't matter. You were still you, just a bit different to anyone else. Let's face it. I was nine years old and wearing a nappy and proud of it.

As we played with not a care in the world, we asked if we could stay up longer.
"Go on, then," Sue answered.

I think as we were the only ones in, she needed the company. I just enjoyed it while I could. I wet my nappy with not a care in the world and we continued to play games and Sue brought us in crisps, chocolate and pop.

"I'll get shot if your mum finds out Ben."

I just laughed and said, "She won't find out, will she, Sue?"

"Of course not, love," and with that, we just kept playing.

Sue asked if we wanted to watch some TV. Not much was on, but I think she wanted to calm us down. We both sat on the settee next to her, one on either side sat watching TV for a bit. I was loving it. Sue asked me if I was okay a couple of times, as I think being a mum, had sussed that I might have had a wee or two, as my nappy was looking a bit different and not as fluffy and puffed out like when she first put it on. I'd wet my nappy about three times, not big ones, just enough to make the needing a wee urge go away and I didn't care about it at all.

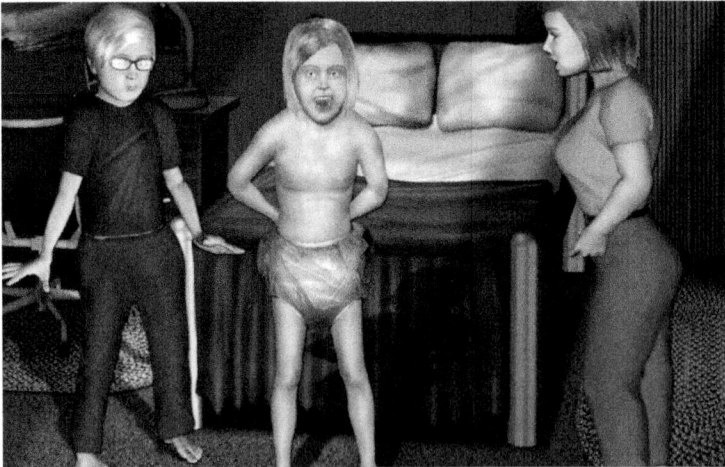

The scene after Sue had finished and Scot walked in. We were all laughing about my situation and that was a good feeling.

It was soon time for bed and as we were going upstairs, Sue whispered to me, "Have you used your nappy yet? You haven't been to the toilet since I put it on. You don't need changing before bed, do you?"

Now what I should have said was, 'Yes' I needed a nappy change, as I loved her doing it before, but I didn't. I wasn't sure if Sue had liked doing nappies again and wanted to change me or if she was just checking.

"I have used it," I explained. "But it's okay".

As we lay in our beds, Scot was asking me what it was like to wear a nappy at our age. I couldn't really answer him in an honest way, as I didn't know what to say. I just said that it felt different and sometimes it was okay and other times not.

"Is it smelly when you wee?"

We both started giggling. "Er, no not really as I take it off as soon as I can."

We both soon fell asleep and didn't wake up until about nine the following morning. Scot's mum came in soon after.

"Good morning boys!" she chirped. "Come on get up, breakfast is ready."

She left the room and Scot and I both got out of bed. Scot still had his pyjamas on, and I was only wearing my top. I didn't even bother putting any bottoms on. I just put some socks on and we both went downstairs to the kitchen. I had been sitting a few minutes when I realised that as I had used my nappy prior to bed, it now felt very wet and a bit uncomfortable. We had some cereal and toast and then Sue asked us what we wanted to do for the morning till I had to go home. We couldn't use the swimming pool as it wouldn't be ready until dinner time as Sue had only just turned the heater up when she got up. So, Scot and I agreed to play in the garden till it was time for me go home.

"Right Scot, go and get washed and dressed and brush your teeth and give me a shout when you're out of the bathroom."

Scot went upstairs, leaving me and Sue at the table.

"I'll help you when Scot's finished in the bathroom, Ben, if you want. You will probably need a shower or something."

"Okay," I replied, quite accepting of the fact that Sue would help me.

It was about fifteen minutes or so when Scot shouted down. We had been talking about my family members up north and how it had been a long time since we had seen them. The subject only came up as she was talking about Scot's grandparents, which was where Sophie and her dad had gone the previous day.

"Right, come on now. Nappy time!"

We went upstairs into the bathroom, where I removed my top ready for a shower. I had been able to take my nappy off by myself already, so I pulled down the plastic pants and unpinned my nappy. I was holding onto it, as I didn't want to put it on the bath mats that were laid out.

"Give them to me, love. I'll sort them out." Sue took the wet nappy and pants from me and remarked with a laugh, "Blooming heck, Ben! This is a very wet one!"

"They are in the morning, as I'm not allowed to use the toilet," I explained.

I jumped into the bath and had a good wash down, got out and after a quick dry down, wrapped a huge towel around my whole body and went out onto the landing.

"Is that better now, Ben?"

"Yes," I replied.

Scot was in his room and was nearly dressed by now.

"Ben, mum said we can make a den in the garden today if we want."

"Sure thing!" I replied excitedly, as I loved building dens. My brothers and I did that often, using anything we could get our hands-on.

"Hurry up and get dressed. I'll meet you outside," and with that, Scot bolted off down the stairs.

I went into Scot's room where Sue had put my clothes out ready for me. I was soon dressed and heading out to the garden. As I went out through the door, the familiar sight on the washing line was in full view. Two nappies and two pairs of plastic pants blowing about drying. Scot's mum had washed them and was getting them dry for me to put in my bag. Scot had started to get some chairs out and blankets ready to build the den.

"Come on Ben, we can use these to make a massive den."

I grabbed another blanket and a chair and moved it all to the centre of the garden, ready to build.

Scot then said, "Haven't you got your nappy on today? I thought you had to wear it all the time?"

"No," I said.

"Ah okay," Scot replied.

I was stunned a little as to why he'd said it to be honest, so I replied, "Why? Has your mum said something?"

"Nah, nothing, I just thought you liked having a nappy on like last night."

"Ahh yeah I did, didn't I!".

We were both laughing as Sue brought us a drink of pop out.

"What you two laughing at then?"

"Nothing," we both said at the same time while holding our peace about the nappy question.

"Your den's looking good, boys. Are girls allowed in it?"

"No way!" Scot shouted out loud.

"That's not fair!" Sue said, with a broad smile on her face.

We finished our den and were having a really good time when Sue came out and said, "Ben, time to go home in a bit, love."

"Okay, Sue," I shouted from the den.

Scot then asked, "Do you have to put a nappy back on?"

"Yeah, else mum will shout, and I'll be in trouble."

We played for another ten minutes or so until Sue came out again.

"Ben, come on now."

I exited the den we had just built and went into the house. Scot was still playing in the den until it was time to go.

"I've brought your stuff down, Ben. It's in the front room."

"Okay, thank you," I replied.

"Ben... You've got to put a nappy back on now. You know that, don't you?"

"Yeah, mum said I had to," I replied.

"Come on then and I'll help you, if you want me to?"

"Sure!"

I grabbed the nappy Sue had laid out for me and put it on the floor. I took off my shorts and underpants and lay down as near to the middle of the nappy as I could. Sue then knelt on the floor and pulled up the towelling between my legs, fixing it firmly into place with the pins. She grabbed the plastic pants and wriggled them up my legs and over my nappy and made sure everything was tucked in.

"There you go, Ben!" she said with a smile.

I got back up and put my shorts back on and then waited while Sue went to tell Scot to put his shoes on, as we were going.

We were soon heading home, and I was so happy. I'd had a great night and Sue had been really kind about the nappies. Scot was good about it as well. I was a little surprised about that, but he was a nice person anyway. His whole family were. As we entered the shop, it was rather busy, so we went upstairs where mum was making ironing. She was happy to see me home again.

"Hi, Ben! Did you have had a nice time?"

"Brilliant!" I replied.

"Sue, any problems?"

"None at all. He was good as gold. I've washed the nappies and they are in his bag."

"Sue, you shouldn't have done that," she offered.

"It was fine. Not a problem."

I said thank you to Sue and Scot for having me and as they left, Sue shouted, "See you tomorrow at school, Di!"

I got a drink of pop and asked mum what was for tea then went upstairs to my room where Alex was playing with his toys. We carried on playing until it was time for tea. After tea, we helped clear the pots then mum told me to go into the front room.

"Alex, go and see if Andrew wants a cup of tea, please.

Alex disappeared, and mum came in carrying a nappy.

"Lie down please."

I just did it, no questions, no bother. I laid on the floor while mum changed my nappy again. I thought it would be over by now, but obviously, I was wrong. I stood up and pulled my t-shirt down and mum said to go and play while she picked my shorts up and the wet nappy she'd just removed. I went upstairs and carried on playing until Alex came back up. Alex then asked if I wanted to go to the field nearby. There was a small wood there and we played armies and games like that.

"Mum, can we play out for a bit please?"

"Yes, but back in for eight o'clock, please. It's school tomorrow and Ben, put your shorts on if you're going out, okay?"

I grabbed a pair of shorts and did my best to conceal my nappy. Alex and I then headed out to the field.

Steve was there with his mates and it didn't take long for one them to shout, "He's got a nappy on!"

"Hey, Ben! Do you need your nappy changed?" another shouted.

I tried to ignore them, but it was hard to do. Alex and I headed for the wood and played armies until it was time to go home. On the way home, we passed my brother and his mates again. They were all laughing and pointing at me. I was really embarrassed and tried to walk a bit quicker to get away from them.

"Hey, Ben! Why are you out now? Shouldn't you be in bed now? Only babies wear nappies!"

They all started laughing again and I just carried on with my head down, trying not to listen. We soon got home and went upstairs where mum was. She told Alex to get undressed and go for a shower then put his pyjamas on.

"You're next Ben, so don't go far please."

As soon as Alex was out, I was called back as it was my turn. I went into the bathroom and took my nappy off which was wet now and got in the shower. Mum came in and picked up the wet nappy and plastic pants and took them out. Once I had finished, I dried off as best I could and then wrapped a towel around myself so that mum could dry my hair and so on. I went into the living room where Alex was sitting watching TV in his pyjamas.

"Come here, Ben. Let's dry your hair."

Mum always brought the hairdryer down from her room, so she could watch TV while sorting us out. When mum had finished, I stood up and she helped dry me off properly. She reached behind her and pulled out a nappy and plastic pants.

"Lie down, Ben."

Once again, I just did it. As she was putting my nappy on this time, she said, "Right Ben, this is the last time I expect to be putting you in nappies. If this nappy is dry in the morning you can go back to underpants, okay?"

"Yes, mum. Thank you."

"If I ever catch you doing this again, we will go back to nappies and for a lot longer, do you understand me?"

"Yes," I replied.

"Right. Put your top on."

She had left my bottoms upstairs on purpose, so as usual, I was just wearing a t-shift pyjama top and with a bloody big nappy on view.

Mum came in on Monday morning to get us up for school. I got out of bed and was confident my nappy was still dry, as I'd been to the toilet during the night instead of using it. I ran downstairs and asked mum if I could take my nappy off.

"Hang on, Ben. Have your breakfast first. Another five minutes won't hurt, will it?

I ate my breakfast and then for the last time, mum pulled my plastic pants down and made sure I hadn't wet it.

"Right," she said, and she pulled them back up again. "Go and take it off and put it in the washing basket and remember what I said, Ben. And I mean it!"

"Yes, mum," I replied, and went to the toilet and took it off.

I went to school that day knowing that I wouldn't be put back in a nappy later on when I got home. By the time I had gotten home, the nappies had all been put away and probably put back in the garage. All I know is that this experience had made me not want to wear nappies at all. Although while a couple of times I didn't mind it, the embarrassment, having to use it and being made to wear it with no trousers on for a whole week had taken its toll. Also, the fact that mum changed my nappies was embarrassing too, especially when others were around. The ribbing stopped after about two months and it mainly happened when adverts came on TV advertising disposable nappies, as they were getting popular in the '80s.

"Ben, you're on TV again!" and things like that.

It soon passed though, and things went back to normal. I didn't really think about nappies for the next three years or so. I didn't get the urge to wear one and it completely vanished in my mind. Little did I know that it had just gone away for a rest, so to speak. This thought would never go away completely, and it was just a matter of time before it reappeared in my head.

This was my pre-teen nappy experience, and this is the first time I've spoken or written about it, for obvious reasons. I'd found out that if you have a good friend who you trust, you can tell them anything and they accept you for who you are, weird or not. Scot never did tell anyone and never made fun of me in the time that I knew him. He was such a great friend and to this day, I regret not keeping in touch with him and his family. But at that age, time doesn't matter, and after moving again and finding another friend, I suppose kids move on. Sue also was great and was the first adult that had allowed me to express myself, but even she didn't understand completely… or maybe she did?

It is not easy to explain something you do or feel when it's not classed as "normal". Mind you, what is normal?

Fear and Joy – a life in and out of nappies ▎

One person's *normal* is another person's weird and vice versa. Sue did ask me on a couple of occasions if I'd worn a nappy again, to which I was always able to say no. We would talk a little about it, but I didn't understand really, and I think Sue was trying her best to understand why or how I was feeling about it. At my age though, I wasn't very patient and got a bit embarrassed at times knowing that Sue had actually put a nappy on me. So, was it wrong what I did, thinking about it now? No, I don't think so anyway. What's wrong with it? Weird, yes; acceptable, sort of maybe. But most people wouldn't understand unless they were experiencing the thoughts I was having at the time. If I was to say to you at age nine, I have a desire to wear a nappy, you would probably think, why? Why would you want to wear a nappy? But in the same context if you replied to me that you wanted to wear girl's clothes, would I say the same thing? Why? Why would you want to wear girl's clothes? It's the same thought or desire. It's just individual and only that individual understands or doesn't understand why they have these desires and thoughts to do or wear certain things. It must be programmed in us and our own desires and thoughts are what makes us all different and as long as we are not harming anyone, who has the right to judge or make fun?

No one.

Chapter 3 - Age 13 – 24

H ere I was – thirteen years of age and thankfully, my parents had decided to move back up north.

This was brilliant, as I hated living down south for those few years. We didn't fit in at all being northerners and along with my two brothers, my mum also yearned to move back. We moved to a semi-nice area, and I went to a half-decent good school. My life pretty much went as any other 13-year-old teenager does. Some of the schools down south were very rough and before moving back north, my brothers and I had started smoking, were committing minor shop thefts (sweets and cigarettes and so on, nothing serious), and along with my two brothers, were always in some kind of trouble - even with the police!

At age thirteen, if money was short, I was rolling my own ciggies! Thankfully, we never got arrested or anything like that. It was normally that our cigarettes would be confiscated or if we had damaged some property, often by falling through the roofs of garages we were climbing on, then we would be taken back to our house where the police would explain the matter and leave it with my parents to deal with. The punishment was normally a really good backside thrashing, and I mean hard, followed by early to bed every night for a week and not allowed out and other similar punishments. Those bottom smacks stung for a few hours, let me tell you!

The area in Manchester we moved back to.

Manchester in the early '80s

Following the punishment I received before, my desire to wear any form of nappy or trainer pants been completely put to the depths of my mind. Although some of it was fun, the majority was so embarrassing, it has stayed with me to this day. This had all been forgotten by now and was never mentioned again by anyone. I think mum thought - or hoped – that it was just a phase I was going through. To be honest, I wished she was right and that it was only a phase. It would have saved me a lot of turmoil and low self-esteem throughout the following years of my life.

At this point, I hadn't thought about nappies for about four years, nor did I have the desire to put one on. Life for me was pretty much like any child in their first year as a teenager. I had some good mates, was pretty much left to my own devices along with my brothers and I suppose, given the area we lived in and the lack of income into the house, life was okay. Nothing to write home about, but nothing to complain about either.

After moving back up north to Manchester, I had been able to secure a paper round job which gave me some pocket money each week. We didn't get any pocket money from home, except maybe a £1 at weekends, if we were going to the local youth club. Being a smoker, it was a good job that ciggies were not as expensive as they are today. A packet of twenty would last me a while and all three of us usually shared a pack of smokes, clubbing together to buy a pack, smoke and pass a lit ciggy about.

Our cigarettes of choice at the time were B&H, Gold Mark (99p for 20) or JPS in the black box, also known as lung busters. We had all been caught smoking at various intervals. Punishment was harsh and strict, as our stepdad was very old fashioned, having been brought up with strict discipline himself, something which he made my mum do to us. As we grew older, I think we were becoming tired of him, but he knew what he was getting into when he married my mum, so it was his own fault if he started regretting it.

To our delight, we had also been back in contact with my dad again who was now married to Jackie. She was such a lovely lady and had tamed my dad a bit. We were always welcome at the house and she made us feel at home whenever we went. Up until the day she died, she put up with my dad and always made time for us if we went over. Visiting dad was great, as we also got to see our grandparents who loved us very much and missed us a lot when we were stopped from visiting for all those years. We tried to make up for it, but you can't get back the early years of a child's life, so we just made the most of it. I later found out that there was a lot of bravado and tit for tat between my parents and stepdad. We children were normally the pawns in their silly childish games. I never forgave any of them for that, although I do know my stepdad was a major player in these games.

So, what happened at this stage of my life to leave an imprint on my memory - either for good or for bad?

Our favourite brand choice of ciggies, as they were cheap.

It was 1983/4 and end of year exams had just started at school. I hated school and disliked exams even more. I never studied, and I would just wing it. I was more interested in getting out of school at the end of the day, having a smoke and messing about on the way home. I was never asked if I had homework, so consequently, I didn't do any and was always in trouble for it at some point during the week. This normally meant detention or catching up during breaks, but thankfully, I always had a mate in detention, so it wasn't that bad. Exam time meant that the end of the school year was approaching, and the six-week summer holiday was approaching - something I lived for, as this long holiday was always great.

On weekdays during the holidays, I could start my paper round early, as I wasn't at school. As I was starting early, I could take my time with it, so I walked instead of doing it on my bike. While walking, I would chat with the adults I delivered papers to, especially the elderly ones. I always respected my elders and loved their stories about the war and so on. My younger brother and I did join Cubs and we lasted for...a whole night. We were expelled for being too troublesome and causing havoc in the local scout hut. This didn't go down well at all and on return home, we were administered the obligatory smacked behind several times by my mum until it stung.

About halfway around my route, I normally went to the end of the road and cut back into the next street, but as I was walking, I could use the back footpath as a shortcut. As I walked down the pathway, reading a comic that someone had ordered for their kid to be delivered with their evening paper, my eye was drawn to a similar sight from my past. It was a washing line in someone's garden.

It was full of terry nappies and plastic pants! I hadn't seen this sight for years, and as it was the 80's, disposable nappies were cheaper and getting more popular, so washing nappies and hanging them out were fairly rare now.

I just looked and couldn't help but think back to my younger days. I must have stopped about thirty seconds or so when a man from the garden opposite asked me if I was okay. I just said I was waiting for a friend and I carried on through the path to the next street. While delivering the papers and on my way back to the shop, I couldn't stop thinking about those nappies and plastic pants on the line. My brain was working overtime and I couldn't understand why. I soon forgot about it and went home for my tea, as we always did at about 6 pm. I carried on for the rest of the day as normal and thankfully, didn't give the nappies any more thought.

As I look back now, I see that a part of my brain was probably hard-wired to this type of thought or desire and while up until now it had gone to sleep, it was now starting to awaken. The next day, I did the same route on foot and as I passed the same spot for some reason, I was hoping to see the same view, but I didn't, and I didn't know whether to feel disappointed or happy. I really didn't know how to feel. I was now thirteen years old and a growing lad, but half a dozen nappies and plastic pants on a washing line had stopped me in my tracks. It's not like it was a lovely lady in a bikini with massive gazongers (as we used to call them). That I could understand, but not this. I was really confused and did everything I could to get it out of my head. I finished my round as normal and went home for tea, but this image kept popping back into my head.

Why? Why that image and why now? What was my brain trying to tell me? Thankfully that night, my mates and I had a good laugh while out and about and nappy thoughts soon stopped bugging me and I forgot about them.

A couple of days or more passed and as I was going out, mum asked me to call at a neighbour's house as she needed a favour or something. I can't remember exactly what it was. I said I would do and off I went calling at Margaret's house on the way.

"Hello Ben, come in, dear," she announced, as I arrived.

"Hiya, Margaret. Mum said you needed me for a job."

Margaret was divorced with no kids and lived alone. I did favours for her quite often, as I always helped people if they need it. I'm the same even today. Margaret was about 45-50 years old (I think). I never asked, but she looked older than my mum, anyway. She drank a bit, smoked like a chimney and to me, always looked pleased to see someone. I guess she must have been lonely as she didn't get out much. To this day I can't remember what I had to do. It must have been something simple like move a piece of furniture or put the bins out, which I regularly did for her. I was her favourite, as she always asked my mum for me to help her. I would sometimes sit for a couple of hours chatting away about all kinds of things. After a cup of tea and a crafty smoke (Margaret let me smoke in her house), she asked me if I'd nip to the local shop and get her some more ciggies.

"Yeah, no problem," I said.

"And get ten for yourself lovey, but don't tell anyone," she offered cheerily.

"Ahh cheers, Margaret, I won't," and off I went to the shop, which was about a half-mile away.

It was a nice day as usual with loads of people out playing. It took ages to get to the shop, as I kept stopping to talk to friends and so on. Eventually, I reached the little mini-market shop. There were a few customers in, so I just had a look about. It needed to be empty as the shop keeper would sell me the cigarettes only if he or she knew they were for Margaret. The shop keeper was a lovely Asian lady and her husband from time to time would also make an appearance. There was always the smell of cooking going on and it always made me hungry. As I was wandering around waiting, I suddenly spotted a large pink and blue striped box around the corner shelving unit. It read 'PVC Baby Pants Sizes S-XL'.

My first thought was to wonder if that meant plastic pants.

No one could see me, so I peered inside. I was right. There, inside the box were about twenty pairs of plastic pants of all sizes! They were the same type I had worn in my early years, same colour and look. All at once, the past memories raced through my mind, along with the feeling I had when I first tried on those trainer pants back when I was nine.

It felt like I stood there for ages, but it was only a second. I walked away and carried on looking at the shelves, hoping no one had seen me. There were only a couple of customers left, so I knew I would be able to get the ciggies soon. I started to wonder if the pants would fit me, guessing that the XL ones might, so I headed back to see if I could see a price. I had a couple of pounds on me from my paper round wages, so I might be able to afford a pair. They were £1.49 ish and I knew I could afford a pair.

The thoughts kept rushing to and fro through my head... "Do I buy them? Don't buy them! Buy them!"

This went on for five minutes until the last customer was served. I went up to the counter and spoke to the lady.

"Margaret has sent me for two packets of cigarettes, please."

"Okay, seeing as they are for her, I will serve you," she replied.

She tilled up the ciggies, I handed over the money and collected my change. I put the cigs in my pocket and left the shop. I immediately thought to myself that I'd forgotten to buy mine, which she said I could have for going. I turned back and went into the shop, but as soon as I entered, I went straight to the lady at the counter.

"Excuse me, do you have a pair of the XL baby pants, please? I forgot to ask before."

She looked at me and said, "I'm not sure," and headed towards the shelf where they were.

She lifted the box off the shelf and peered inside, "Yes, we do. How many would you like?"

"Just one, please," I replied.

She brought them back and put them on the counter and rung them up in the till. I can't remember exactly what price they were, but I got change from £2.

"Thank you," I said and stuffed them in my pocket and left the shop.

I kept my hand in my pocket, ensuring that the pants did not fall out or anything and started on the journey back to Margaret's.

All the way there I kept thinking, "Would they fit?"

"Why did I buy them?"

"Would they fit me properly?"

And then there was the question of what else I could have spent the money on. The questions just raced around in my head all the way back. I had a feeling of excitement at the fact I had them in my pocket and how soon would it be before I could try them on. I also now realised that I'd forgotten my ciggies too, but as I had a couple stashed away, I'd be okay. How ironic is it that at the same I was thinking about having a smoke, I was also clutching a pair of plastic pants in my pocket so that they don't fall out. Talk about two thoughts being worlds apart, these were a universe apart and I had no idea why. To me it made no sense at all and I just had to accept that.

Buying my first pair of plastic pants!

On return to Margaret's house, I gave her the cigs and asked if she wanted me to make her a brew.

"Thanks, Ben, and yes, that would be nice if you're stopping for a cup as well?" she replied.

"Yeah, I'll have a brew. I'll just go to the loo first."

I went to the loo upstairs and locked the door and double-checked that it would not open. I then knelt on the floor and pulled out the plastic pants, opening them up to have a proper look. I can remember the smell they gave off, a smell which is the same today and the same from my early years. They were soft to the touch and although they were XL baby size, they looked like they would fit.

I undid my trousers and pulled them down, so I could see if they might fit by holding them up to my waist. I was in luck. It did look as though they would fit me. I took my shoes off and removed my trousers completely. I made sure though that I didn't make too much noise, listening for anyone coming up the stairs. I slipped the pants over my feet and started to pull them up. All was going well, but they were harder to pull up. Eventually, I managed to pull them up over my underpants and into position. They were a bit tight, but they were on. The feeling was... well... I can't describe it really, but I liked it.

A lot.

I looked at them as they covered my coloured underpants. Not quite the old look I had when younger, but it was more than fine. I quickly pulled on my trousers and slipped my shoes back on, flushed the loo then headed downstairs. As I walked, I could feel the plastic pants as they were a little snug around my waist and the tops of my legs, but I could feel them, so I was happy. I went into the kitchen and made the brews, taking them into where Margaret was, and I sat down with her. She offered me a ciggie which I kindly took, and I sat down in the chair with a look like the cat that got the cream.

Again, I thought, "Why have I done this and what would anyone have said if they saw me having a smoke knowing I'm wearing plastic nappy pants?"

But at the time, I couldn't have cared what anyone thought, I was just content with what I was doing.

Trying the plastic pants on in Margaret's bathroom.

An hour or so passed, and I thought I'd better go, as I said I'd meet my mate, Alan earlier. I made my excuses and asked to use the loo again, as I needed to take these pants off. I checked to make sure the loo door was locked, and I took off the pants putting them in my pocket, flushed the toilet, then headed downstairs. Now, as I had been caught before and had faced the punishment for having worn nappies, I quickly thought that I must find somewhere to hide them. Margaret had a garage at the side of her house and I was always in there, so I thought that would be perfect.

"Margaret, can I borrow the bike pump from the garage and I'll bring it back tomorrow?" I asked

"Of course, darling. Help yourself!"

Brilliant I thought. I can now hide these pants and prevent anyone from finding them. If they did, it would be humiliating for me. I went into the garage and found a really good hiding spot and hid the plastic pants wrapped in a plastic bag. Now that they were hidden, I picked up the bike pump and headed out.

"Bye Margaret, see you later. Shout if you need anything," I said, as I departed

I headed out of the front door and made my way to Alan's house about five minutes away. On the way there, I was thinking about the last two hours and was happy. Why was I happy? I've no idea why. I just was. Most kids my age would be happy with a can of beer they shouldn't have or a new toy they have just saved up for and just bought and here I was, the happiest kid on the block, as I'd just bought a pair of plastic nappy pants, tried them on, walked about in them for an hour and was ecstatic about it.

I couldn't understand why I felt like this at all, nor could I talk to anyone about it either. How could I? So, in a way, I was trapped and couldn't express my reasons for being happy, as I knew that no one would understand. I also felt that I must be the only one that does this, as it's not what we would call *normal*. There was no internet, chat room or social media, so I felt lonely and that I must be the only boy aged thirteen in the world that was doing this and I was always asking myself - why me? Why this? But I never got an answer. How could I? I couldn't tell anyone.

I met up with Alan as planned, although a little late and we spent the day messing around and doing things that thirteen-year-old boys do. I soon forgot about earlier and was happy that the thoughts that were confusing me had gone again, for now.

It was soon time to head back for tea and as usual, all the family were together at the table telling each other about their day and so on. My brothers and I cleaned up the plates and then headed back out, as we did every night unless it was raining, in which case we found someone's house to go to. I tried to think of an excuse to go back to Margaret's, but I couldn't. I just wanted to check on my hidden pants and to look at them again. I met up with Alan as planned and we walked the streets, messing about and having a fag whenever we could. It was soon time to head home, as it was getting dark and the signal for home time was the street lights coming on.

Back home, I sat in my room (I had my own room now) thinking about the day. I was thinking of a way to get the pants back here and hidden, but at the same time, images of the last time I was caught with nappies flashed through my mind and there was no way I could go through that again at my age - it would be horrendous. It was bad enough at nine and a total embarrassment and humiliation. It did make me think of the night I stayed at Scot's house and now his mum had been really good about it and the moment we all laughed in Sophie's room. How I wished I could find somebody like that, someone who understood and accepted what I was doing, but still saw that I was a normal kid and that it didn't change who I was.

A few days went by and thankfully Margaret had asked my mum if I could go around and get some boxes out of the loft for her and do a bit of shopping and so on. Great! I thought.

It was a Saturday morning and I headed around and found Margaret in the front garden doing some weeding.

"Hello Ben, thanks for coming, lovey," she said.

"Hiya, want a brew?" I replied.

"Ooh yes please!", she replied with a smile.

I went into the kitchen and started to make the brew and thought that while the kettle was boiling, I could sneak into the garage and check to see if the pants are still there. I went to the hiding place, took out the plastic bag and pulled out the pants and shook them so they opened up. I smiled and thought that I had to try these on again and soon. But for now, I couldn't, so I put them back and headed back to the kitchen to finish making the brews and taking Margaret's out to her.

"What did you want me to do, Margaret?" I asked.

"Oh, can you put the boxes that are at the top of the stairs into the loft for me?"

"Yeah no problem, I'll go and do it now."

I went up the stairs to where the boxes were and moved them to the loft hatch opening. I got the ladders out, got everything into place and then puffed and panted as I lifted the box through the hole.

Once they were both up I climbed into the loft and moved the boxes to the side out of the way of the opening. As I turned around, I noticed a pile of bedding and towels which I suppose were spares. As I looked at the pile, I spotted a white one about halfway down! My brain suddenly went into overdrive and thought mode. I could see that this would work as a nappy under my pants!

I picked it out and threw it down the loft hatch opening. Once I had cleared up, I picked the towel up and opened it out. It was larger than a hand towel but smaller than a bath towel, so I thought to myself that this could work. I didn't have any pins, but then I remembered mum always had some in her sewing box, so I could use them. I folded the towel up and took it out to the garage where I hid it with the plastic pants. As I stuffed the bag into its hiding place, I was thinking to myself that I needed to try that towel on and see if the pants would fit over the top. I went back to the front garden where Margaret was finishing off.

"All done for you," I said.

"Thanks, Ben. You're a love."

We both went into the house and had another brew and a ciggie for me. Then I said I'd have to go, as I was meeting my mates.

"Ok lovey," Margaret said. "See you later and thanks for the help, Ben. You're a little star!"

I met up with Alan as normal and we both went to his house for a bit of dinner then headed off to the park to catch up with our other friends and see what was happening for the rest of the day. It was another fabulous day, not a care in the world and like any other day, I had soon forgotten about nappies again.

It was soon time to head home and during tea, mum said to me and asked, "Have you been to Margaret's yet, Ben?"

"Yes," I replied.

"Good lad. She's a lonely woman, I think. I don't know if she has any family around here," mum said.

"I don't think so either, mum. She smokes likes a chimney though."

"She does Ben, and I think she likes a tipple or two at night as well," mum said, laughing.

"She does mum, yeah. She's a nice lady too. Very friendly and she always thanks me for going around and doing jobs for her. Shame she has no kids of her own to look after her, isn't it?"

"It is love, but some people don't want kids, but at least you go and help her, hey?" Mum replied.

"Yeah, I like going around too, she buys me chocolate," I said. Both mum and I then started laughing.

"You're a good boy.... sometimes," mum said, still laughing. "Right, come on let's get these pots sorted."

After tea, I decided to see if I could find some nappy pins. This would then finish off what I needed to try a full nappy on again. Once everyone had vacated the kitchen, I looked in the cupboard for mum's sewing tin. Bingo! I found two nappy sized baby pins. Not locking ones, but the same size as the ones mum used to use to pin my nappies on. I put them in my pocket and went upstairs to my room, hiding them in my bedside drawer.

A few days went by with nothing really exciting happening. My brothers and I were enjoying the school summer holidays, each hanging about with our own mates and occasionally meeting up somewhere as a group. Andrew was working in Manchester doing imports and mum worked at a local shop and bakery. On this particular Sunday, I had popped around to Margaret's to take a video back that we had borrowed a few nights ago. I sat in the front room with Margaret having a ciggie with my brew and just chatting really. She always talked about her dad, who had died about five years earlier. You could see she was proud of him and missed him dreadfully. Sometimes, she would get photos out of him and show me, which was nice, as it showed the old days and how life was for him, which was just amazing to see how far we had come in the '80s.

Fear and Joy – a life in and out of nappies

As I knew I was going to Margaret's, I took the nappy pins with me, as they were easy to conceal in my pocket to get out of the house. I had been planning for a while to ask if I could use the garage as a den but had never gotten around to it. I now needed to ask so that I could try the nappy on. So, without any more delay, I asked Margaret if I could make a small den in the garage for wintertime, where me and Alan and maybe our other mates could hang out when it was raining and cold.

"What a great idea! I don't use it, so yeah, go ahead, Ben," Margaret said.

"Thanks, Margaret. I'll go and have a look to see what I will need to do," I replied.

"Be careful in there, Ben won't you love. Don't injure yourself."

"I will, I'll tidy it up for you too while I'm doing it, okay?" I said.

"Okay Ben, thanks", Margaret replied and with that, I headed out into the garage.

As I got in there, my first thought was to look for a place to lie down and try my nappy on, now that I had everything I needed. I made some room on one side of the floor and threw about four blankets on the floor after sweeping up. I pulled out the bag with the towel and pants in and put them on the blanket. I then put a block on the garage door handle, so nobody could just walk in. It was perfect, I thought. I took my shoes and trousers off and lay on the blanket. Once I had the towel into the position I removed my underpants and pulled the towel up between my legs and pulled both the sides round pinning them in place.

The feeling was something I can't describe, and I remember thinking at the time, "Why did this feel nice and so normal to me?"

Once the towel was comfy and pinned correctly, I reached for the plastic pants, putting them over my feet and started to pull them up. I struggled for a bit, but eventually, the pants went over the towel and I stood up. It was like going back in time and here I was wearing a nappy again, but thirteen years old.

I lifted my t-shirt to get a proper look and I smiled as I saw the pins making a shape on the plastic pants, as they were a bit tight on. I started walking around the garage and to me, it felt normal. I've no idea why it felt normal to me. It just did, and I felt very happy.

I then sat on the blanket and looked around the garage to see how I was going to make this den. I stayed in the garage for about half an hour before I decided to take the nappy off. Once I had taken the nappy off and got dressed, I put it back in the bag and hid it. I went back to the house feeling wonderful and happy and was already planning when I could return to do it again. It had felt good putting a nappy on after all this time. I don't know why it felt this way. It just did. I think the fact that this time the decision to wear a proper nappy was mine helped a little, as it wasn't a punishment, and nobody was going to see me. It was my secret and it would stay that way.

A few days later, I was working on the den when I got to a point where I needed a rest. I had made a seating area and had brought some lunch, as Margaret had gone out for the day visiting friends. She had left me a key to the garage under the mat so that I could come and go as I pleased. As I sat there, I suddenly got the urge to put the nappy on again. As before, I got the bag from its hiding place and put the nappy on. I took my t-shirt off so that the only thing I had on was a nappy. It felt great. I wasn't feeling any guilt or shame, as I was in my den, wearing a nappy by my own choice.

I sat in the chair I had been given for the den and just felt completely at ease, relaxed and happy. Why though? Why would wearing a nappy at thirteen make me feel this way?

I didn't have the answer, nor could I work out why I wanted to put a nappy on at that particular moment, but I had, and I was enjoying it. I reminded myself I was not hurting anyone doing this, although it must be weird if people knew I was doing this. I didn't know anybody else that did and I couldn't ask anyone either, so I was trapped. I honestly thought I was the only thirteen-year-old in the world wearing a nappy, except for those kids that have to wear them for medical reasons.

I had some more boxes to shift and stack, so I put my t-shirt and trainers back on and carried on. I didn't put any trousers on, as I liked the feeling of my nappy being uncovered and it was comfier. As I did the last box, I was beginning to need the loo. If Margaret was out, I'd normally use the grid outside and then put disinfectant down it that she had left out. Then it dawned on me, I've got a nappy on, I could use it like I used to! Without a second thought, I let go and weed in my nappy for the first time. It felt really weird. I had major thoughts of guilt and shame, but at the same time, I was happy I had done it. This was confusing for a thirteen-year-old, I can tell you.

As I carried on, I could see the wet patch start to form on the inside of the plastic pants. The pants were tight and showed everything from the outline of the pins to the wet towel I now had on. Once I had finished, I sat back down and felt the front and back of the nappy to see how much of the towel was wet. It was totally soaked. I'd forgotten now that being older meant longer wees.

I stayed in the nappy for about another half hour before deciding to take it off and head home for the day. I removed the plastic pants, unpinned the nappy and it fell to the floor. I washed off as best I could with the bottle of water I had and then dried myself and got dressed. Now the problem hit me. What do I do with the wet nappy on the floor? I panicked a bit, as I couldn't take it home. I couldn't get into Margaret's and I definitely didn't want to throw it away, as I may want to do this again in a few days. My final decision was to wrap it up in a separate bag, hide it and come back tomorrow and sort it out. I left the garage and headed home with a guilty feeling at what I had just done. My thoughts were always the same at this moment.

Why? Why do I want to do this?

Why did I wet it, surely just wearing it was enough?

I didn't know why, and I couldn't understand this behaviour, only the fact that it was a very strong desire over which I had no control.

The next day, I headed straight to the den, said a quick hello to Margaret then took out the towel and plastic pants and ran back to my house where I managed to wash it in the sink with some bubble bath and shampoo. I was now really regretting using it the previous day and hated this bit, it was like I was seven again and was made to wash my nappies every time I took them off during the punishment phase years earlier. Once they were washed, I put them back in a clean carrier bag and headed back to Margaret's. Once in the den I placed the towel on some boxes to dry and wiped the pants as best I could and put them back in the hiding place. I then went into Margaret's for a brew and a ciggie.

What a nightmare that was!

Here I was at thirteen, planning how to get a nappy washed and dry - not the usual to-do list for a lad my age. Margaret asked me how the den was coming along, while also telling me about her recent short trip to see her friend in Lytham St. Anne's the other day. She said it was a beautiful place. The beaches were lovely and she had enjoyed a catch up with one of her best friends. In a way, I felt sorry for her. She was a kind lady and always smiled and I don't think I ever saw her in a bad mood the whole time I knew her.

I remarked that it sounded like a really nice place and similar to Blackpool to which she said, "Oh Ben, it's a far nicer beach and a much more relaxed place."

"I'd love to go", I replied.

"Come next time I go lovey, you're more than welcome!"

"Don't know if my mum would let me," I replied.

By this I really meant Andrew. He had turned into a real pain and got worse as time went on. No matter what we did, it always had to be approved by him and I mean *everything*.

We would ask mum if we could go somewhere or do something and it was always, "Ask Andrew if it's okay".

A few times I felt like saying to mum, "You can make a decision you know! We are *your* children!" But there was no point.

The answer was usually 'no', or 'maybe' or the worst thing was that we would get the third degree on why we wanted to go somewhere or do something. Most times it was just easier not to do anything, or if we did do it without permission, just do it and hope not to get caught. I ended up explaining this to Margaret, who had already sussed out what Andrew was like, as had most of my friends and thankfully, said that the next time she saw my mum, she would ask if I could go with her to keep her company.

"Thanks, Margaret," I replied. "I hope they say yes."

A few days passed and thankfully for me, any nappy thoughts I had were not overpowering any ideas I had for the next few days. I had been to Margaret's a couple of times for a brew and to go to the shops for her, but did not go and check on my secret stash. On return home from a friend's house after a day of being a nuisance to most households in the local area, mum told me that Margaret had been up to ask if I could go with her to St Anne's next week.

"Can I go please mum?" I pleaded. "It's okay with me Ben, but you'll have to ask Andrew if it's okay to go," she replied.

"Ahh mum, can't you just make the decision? I don't like asking him. He always says 'no'," I said.

"Well, you're going to have to ask him. It's that simple".

Later after tea, I approached Andrew and asked the question. I dreaded asking him anything, as this meant question after question.

"I'll see," was Andrew's response.

That meant he was exerting his authority over me and personally, I think he loved this power trip. Granted, he was in authority, but to question and interrogate every little single thing either I or my brothers wanted to do was torture and it was sometimes easier to just not ask in the first place. About two hours or so passed before he agreed I could go.

"Thank you", I replied.

I really wanted to say something else but didn't dare! So, I had a couple of days before we went, but I was really excited and I ran straight away to let Margaret know.

"Ah that's great Ben," she replied.

The following morning, I was making my way round to my mate's house when I passed a large chemist that was advertising new types of disposable nappies. I stopped for a moment and wondered to myself if there were any other sizes of plastic pants that would possibly fit me better. I have no idea why I suddenly had this thought, nor why I stopped in the first place. It was as if the nappy thought was lurking in my brain, waiting for the right moment to make itself known again. I should have called this thought 'the nappy monster', as it certainly had a way of sneaking up on me. I tried to ignore it, but I couldn't. I was at the mercy of my thoughts yet again.

I plucked up the courage and walked in where a nice lady behind the counter asked if I needed any help. I think the fact she asked me straight away meant that I did not have me any time to consider what I was going to ask and even if I should ask in the first place.

"Hi, do you sell plastic nappy pants that are made for older kids please?"

There, I'd asked. It didn't even feel out of place asking it either.

She replied, "Mmm I'm not sure. I'll just have a look."

She went over to the baby section area where she rifled through a few items before pulling out a long, shaped box.

"We have these, they are for toddler and upwards," she stated.

"Is that the largest ones you have?" I replied.

"It is sorry. How old is the child?"

I stumbled for a minute before replying "Seven. It's my cousin who's coming to stay and still wets the bed."

She brought them back to the counter and opened the box pulling out the plastic pants.

She opened them up and said, "These should be fine. I think they are quite big."

I looked at the opened pair of plastic pants now on view and she was right. They were a lot bigger than the ones I had previously bought.

"How much are they please?" I asked. "£1.99", she replied.

I asked her if she could keep them to one side and I would go home and get some money from my mum. I left the shop and headed home to see how much spending money I had left, taking into account what I would need for the trip. I emptied my money out onto my bed and counted it up. I remember I had about £5.

Normally a boy my age would be thinking of so many other things to spend their money on, but there I was, seeing if I had enough to buy a child-size pair of plastic nappy pants!

Once again, the thoughts of 'why me?' would go around and around in my head. Why this? Why not something else? Of all the things that could have been given to me, I'd been given this!

In a way, I felt angry as I knew this was not a normal type of behaviour for a lad of my age, and again I thought I was the only one. This meant that unless I could find someone who understood me, I would be locked in this mind battle forever - and that scared me a bit. I wanted to be normal like everyone else, even though I was sure that there were other kids my age with strange thoughts or things they did. I even said to myself that there must be another thirteen-year-old wearing nappies, not because they wanted to, but because they had to. That made me feel a little better in knowing that I had a choice - I suppose.

I eventually decided that I would buy the pants and so, I headed back to the shop. As I left the chemist with my purchase concealed in a carrier bag, I realised I had to hide them, so I made an excuse and went to see Margaret.

A typical chemist in the 80's

After having a cup of tea and a quick chat with Margaret, I took the pants into the den and hid them with the other pair.

"Perfect!" I thought. It was all sorted and hidden and no chance of being found out.

I left Margaret's and headed to my mate's house. I ran most of it, as I was now late thanks to stopping at the shop. As usual, this turned out to be a normal summer's day larking about and doing things boys of thirteen do when they are bored! I returned home for tea on time where I met up with Alex and Steve as normal and we told each other about our day and had a laugh while we sat at the table waiting for mum to put out our food. Andrew came in and sat down and then out of nowhere demanded to know who had been messing about with the video recorder, as it had not recorded his programme or something.

None of us answered.

"One of you has done it," he said. "Come on, own up."

Steve and Alex and I just looked at each other. I swear we were all thinking the same thing, basically, *'get a life, knob head!'*

We were never allowed to use the video recorder, could not go into his and mum's bedroom without permission, were not allowed to bring friends around for sleepovers and were not allowed up before 10 am on weekends. If mum said be in by 8 he would say 7.30. It got steadily worse from age ten up until we all left home, which is what he wanted anyhow.

Anyway, none of us admitted to it so, as per normal Andrew behaviour, he banned us for two weeks from watching TV in the front room. This meant watching anything in our rooms on small black and white portables that had a twist tuning button and an aerial you had to move for each station you changed to, but at least it worked.

A couple of days went by and while working on the den with my mate Alan, Margaret came in with a brew and a sandwich for us both.

"Looking good boys," she noted. "Before you go home Ben, come into the house as I need to give you something for your mum."

"Okay, I will," I replied. Alan and I carried on until it was nearly time to head home for tea. "Catch you later, Alan. I'll see if I can come around to yours after," I said.

As per Margaret's request, I went into the house where Margaret was sitting in the front room.

"Hi Margaret, what am I taking round for mum?" I asked.

"Sit down Ben. Do you want a ciggie?"

"Er, no better not, as I'm going straight home from here," I replied.

"Look, Ben, you know I live here on my own and I've no family. Well, my friend has asked me to move to a flat near her. I'm not sure when I'll be going, but it will be soon."

Margaret's house was a council property so as there was no need to sell, so it was easy for her to move.

"Why? Why don't you stay here? I'll keep coming around, I promise," I replied.

"Oh Ben, I know you would, but I like it in St Anne's and the better air would do my health some good and Brenda and I can keep each other company, as we have been friends since we were children," she explained.

"Oh right," I replied sadly.

I was gutted. I liked Margaret and, in my view, if she had had children she would have been a cool mum. I know she gave us a ciggie and let us smoke, but that was the norm where we lived. It felt just like a few years prior when we had just started to settle and make friends and we would be off again, only this time I was staying. I admit I felt like crying, as I would miss her, and I'd have no den and nowhere on cold wet days to go to.

"You will see what I mean when we go in a few days, just how nice it is, Ben," she said.

"Okay, I understand," I replied.

I didn't understand really, but she was the adult and even if I'd have begged her to stay, it would have made no difference. I said I had to go for tea, but I'd come around after, and I headed back where I told my mum what Margaret had just told me.

"Ah that's a shame, but she has to do the best for her Ben, doesn't she?"

"Yeah, I suppose", I replied.

After tea, I headed back round to Margaret's and while having a sneaky ciggie with her, she told me more about the move and why. I told her I was sad about it, which she understood, but she did say I could come and visit anytime I wanted to and that I could bring a mate.

"Can I bring Alan when we go to St Anne's on Friday?" I asked.

"Yeah, of course, Ben," she replied.

"Brilliant! I'll ask him later."

On Wednesday I was around at Alan's, and I asked if he wanted to come with us, which of course he did. His mum agreed straight away, no bother, unlike the time I asked. We told Margaret later that day while we were doing some work in the den. The den was looking good, but we now knew it wouldn't last, so we kind of decided not to do anymore after that day. It was good while it lasted though - particularly for me!

On Thursday morning, Margaret came around to my house to speak to my mum about Friday and everything was sorted straight away with no problems. She explained that Alan was also coming along and was going to see his mum that afternoon. Margaret then asked my mum if I could have a sleepover at hers that night with Alan and watch a video and so on, as she didn't know how long she had left in the area and we were also leaving early tomorrow morning. She said it would also be nice to have a couple of kids to look after before she moved away.

To my great surprise, mum agreed straight away and said, "Oh yes, that would be lovely! What a great idea. Ben, do you want a sleepover?"

"Yeah!" I replied excitedly.

We weren't allowed sleepovers that often, as Andrew usually said we had to come home. You'd think he'd want to get rid of us, but I think he liked the fact that he had the control and didn't want us to see the way other people lived too often. If I went to friends' houses, the parents were cool, and got involved with their kids, didn't question literally everything they did or wanted to do and didn't rule with an iron fist, and more importantly, made me feel welcome - something which Andrew never did with my mates. My mum was okay with my friends, but Andrew was a complete moron and normally embarrassed us in some way if he could.

So, I met with Alan after dinner and he told me that his mum had agreed to a sleepover. We were both so excited and looking forward to watching a video, staying up late and having a laugh. We had a good day messing about as normal, then before heading home for tea, said that we would meet at Margaret's at about six o'clock. Andrew gave me the normal grilling and interrogation about what was happening and so on. I just said quite simply that Alan and I were staying over at Margaret's to watch a film and spend some time with her before she moved and then we were heading off to St Anne's early morning.

In other words - and how I wished I could have said it - "It's just a sleepover and trip out for goodness sake! Chill out!"

After tea, I went and packed my overnight bag, PJs, clothes for the next day, toothbrush and a couple of packs of Top Trumps - a game I loved as a kid. I emptied what was left of my spending money and put it in my pocket before heading downstairs to say goodbye. As I went into the kitchen, mum gave me a little brown envelope with £5 in it.

"Don't tell Andrew, Ben," she said. "Thanks, mum," I replied and shoved it in my bag.

I said goodbye and headed around to Margaret's. As I went into the living room, there were pop, crisps, chocolate and other party items along with a couple of videos to watch. I was so happy and was eagerly waiting for Alan to turn up, so we could start a film.

I asked Margaret hopefully, "Do we have to go to bed at the normal time?"

"I won't say anything if you don't, wink wink," she replied with a grin.

"Ha-ha, thanks, Margaret. I hope Alan gets here soon."

It was now half six and Alan had still not turned up, so I said to Margaret that I would go and see where he was. It was about a five-minute run, so I set off running and soon arrived at Alan's and he answered the door.

"Come on mate, we got a video ready to watch!" I exclaimed.

"I'm not coming, Ben," he replied.

"Why not?" I asked in surprise.

"Don't want to," he said.

"Oh, come on Alan, it'll be fun!" I countered.

"Nah, I don't want to go to St Anne's either. It'll be boring," he said.

"Right. Okay, I'll see you on Friday after tea then?"

"Yeah ok," Alan said, and with that, I started walking back to Margaret's.

I was sad as I was really looking forward to our little party, I was also wondering if my mum would let me stay over now that Alan wasn't. I got back to Margaret's and told her what Alan had said.

"Ahh, what a shame. Never mind, we can still watch the film, can't we?" she said.

"Yeah, of course. Can I still stay over though?" I replied.

"Course you can Ben, don't be daft!"

My sadness soon lifted, and I was happy to be doing something different.

"More chocolate and treats for us, hey?" Margaret said.

We put the film on and settled down to watch it, while I chomped on chocolate and drank pop, Margaret having a glass of wine and some peanuts. She gave me a ciggie when she lit up and to me, this was great. I understood even at this age, that this isn't real life and

I'm only allowed to do these things because I'm not her son and so on, so I just enjoyed the moment while it lasted. The thing I noticed about Margaret was that as she drank more, she became really funny, laughing and cracking jokes and funny sayings, which made me laugh too.

As the film wore on about halfway through, Margaret stopped the video for a toilet break. When she came back in, I asked if I could have a bit of her wine.

"Er, yeah if you like, or do you want a beer instead?" she replied.

"Mmm, a beer please," I said.

Alan and I normally drank cheap beer or cider when we were at the park or youth club on Fridays and Saturdays. There was always someone that would get it for us and we would share the litre bottle while having a ciggie and chatting with our friends. It was great on Friday and Saturday nights.

She brought a beer in for me and again with a wink she said, "Don't tell your mum, will you? I know you and Alan drink beer, as I've found some empties in the garage."

"Course not", I replied, opening the can of beer and continued to watch the film. This was great I thought. "Can I have another beer please?" I said, having polished off the first one a bit quick as thirteen-year-olds normally do.

"Yes love, they are in the fridge," she replied.

I went to the fridge and grabbed another beer and sat down again to continue watching the film. I thought to myself that Alan would be dead jealous when I told him. At the end of the film, Margaret was a little bit tipsy, as she was laughing more and telling me really stupid jokes, which, although stupid, were very funny.

"Right, what film next Ben?" Margaret asked.

"Er, an action one," I replied.

"Right okay then. Go get your jammies on, and then we can start watching one."

"I don't have to go to bed early, do I?" I enquired hopefully.

"Of course not, Ben", Margaret replied. "I always get jammies on about eight o'clock, as I don't need to go out and it's comfier," she continued.

"Okay then, I'll take my stuff upstairs then."

I went upstairs and unpacked my clothes for tomorrow and put my pyjamas on. I think after nearly two cans of beer in an hour I was feeling a little bit light-headed, just like Margaret, but I was happy and enjoying it. I remember thinking about how this wouldn't happen again as she was moving soon. Ah well I thought, at least I'm having a nice time now.

I went downstairs to the front room, sat down and waited for Margaret to return so we could put another film on, the TV was playing and then it happened!

Our favourite choice of alcohol at weekends.

An advert for disposable nappies came on, the one where it shows a towelling nappy and a disposable in comparison. Straight away, and without warning, the nappy thoughts came racing into my mind. I was feeling a little tipsy myself and I had now opened another can of beer!

"What a perfect night it would be if I put a nappy on," I thought to myself. "I've got one in the garage!"

And then came a sudden rush of excitement as I remembered that my new bigger plastic pants were there too. Without any hesitation and not being able to stop myself, I went into the garage, grabbed the towel, pins and new plastic pants and returned to the house. Margaret had still not come back down, so I quietly went back upstairs and hid them in my bag.

Margaret then shouted, "I won't be long Ben, just taking my face off."

"Okay, no problem," I shouted back.

I realised then that I could put my nappy on right then. I had plenty of time, my pyjamas were baggy and Margaret wouldn't notice, as she's a little bit drunk anyway. I went back to the bedroom and as quickly and quietly as possible, I put a nappy on.

The new plastic pants I had bought were amazing! They fit so much better and went up easily even though I was thirteen and these were made for smaller kids. I pulled on my pyjama bottoms and went downstairs. As I got in the front room I looked down and although I knew what I had on unless you really looked, it wasn't obvious I had a nappy on. It felt really good again to have one on and as before, I had no idea why. I sat on the settee and picked up my can of beer and had a drink.

This was just so amazing to me. Not normal in my opinion, but at that moment, I didn't care at all. Margaret soon came down and started the next film going. I was tucking into some chocolate and Margaret was drinking her wine and eating peanuts and crisps. What a fabulous night I was having, but what about the irony. I was thirteen years old, smoking, drinking a can of beer while pinned into a terry nappy covered with plastic pants.

It made me laugh inside and I thought to myself that only I knew about it. This was is my *thing*, strange though it is and something I had no control over at that time in my life. But in that instant, I was happy and enjoying myself, so was it wrong? I wasn't out causing trouble or doing drugs or any other bad things that went on in my area at the time. I soon finished my second can of beer and was definitely feeling a bit tipsy, but also calm, relaxed and I suppose, content. We were both enjoying the film and by now I was glad that Alan had decided not to come and stay.

I put my empty can down to which Margaret stated, "You can have one more Ben, then that's it, okay?"

"Ok, thanks," I replied and got up to go and get another from the fridge.

I returned from the kitchen, sat down and carried on watching the film. As I sat back down and got into the film I had decided to use the nappy, confident that it would be okay, as I had tried it in the den the last time I put a nappy on. So, without any hesitation, I just weed into my nappy. This is great, I thought! No toilet stops for me. Again, I laughed inside at what I was doing but still thinking if I got caught like this, especially by my mum, the punishment would be really bad.

Margaret paused the film as she needed the loo, so I just went in my nappy again, being careful, as I didn't want it to leak or anything.

On her return, Margaret was carrying a small bottle of whisky.

"You can't beat a whisky, Ben," she said and with that, poured herself a large tumbler of whiskey and coke.

She offered me a taste and I thought it tasted awful. She laughed as I handed her back the whiskey.

"One day you may like it, Ben," she said laughing.

I was laughing too and said, "I'll just drink the beer thanks," and then took a drink from the can to get rid of the taste of the whiskey.

I pressed play on the video and we both sat back and watched the remainder of the film. It was about 10 pm when it finished, and I thought it would be bedtime, but happily, Margaret said if I wasn't tired we could either watch TV or play a game of cards.

I opted for the TV, so Margaret said I could choose another film to watch from the cupboard in the hallway. I got up and after looking for another film, I couldn't find one of interest, so I asked Margaret where the cards were.

"In here love, behind the couch in the drawer," she said.

I went to the drawer, located the cards and sat down again.

As I was taking the cards out, Margaret said, "Ben, I don't mean to embarrass you, but what are you wearing? I noticed something earlier, but didn't like to say anything, as I thought I was wrong."

I was stumped. I think the beer and the relaxing evening had made me drop my guard quite a bit. What would I say, should I be honest or say I needed them for bed.

I trusted Margaret, so I thought it only fair to tell her the truth. I knew she wouldn't say anything and for a split second, I thought of Scot and the night I spent there some years ago.

"Yes, I am Margaret. I've got a nappy on," I replied, a little embarrassed.

"Oh okay, love, do you wet the bed?" she asked.

I lowered my head and answered honestly, "No Margaret, I wear one because I want to, it's wrong I know but-"

Margaret quickly interrupted, "It's alright Ben, don't be ashamed of it, we all have our things we like to do, don't we?"

"Yeah I know, but I'm too old for them, but I can't stop myself from doing it," I replied.

"Well you're not hurting anyone are you, and I must admit I've never known anyone do it before, but it's certainly not wrong, Ben," Margaret stated.

"Thanks, Margaret, I wish I could stop wearing them, but I've tried and it always starts again."

"Well it is what it is love., I'm sure it's difficult for you at your age, but you're not to feel ashamed or embarrassed in this house, okay?"

"Ok, thanks Margaret", I replied.

She then offered me a ciggie which I took quickly and as I sat there puffing away and taking a sip of beer, I felt so much better for telling her the truth and even better as she hadn't mocked me or made fun of it. For the next half hour or so she asked me questions about it and I was as honest as I could be. I told her about my younger days, not in detail, but I think she got the idea of maybe why I liked having a nappy on. She certainly came across as being understanding and for the second time in my life, I had found someone I could talk to about it and be open with them. It is such a relief when you can confide in someone. It's like a weight being lifted off your shoulders, particularly when they tell you that you're are not weird and just a normal kid. I must have been feeling the effects of the beer, as I asked Margaret if I could wear a nappy on the car journey the next day.

"Of course, you can if you want to, darling," Margaret replied. "Look, Ben, you're still the same person love. If wearing a nappy makes you happy then you wear it tomorrow, okay?"

"Okay," I replied.

"Right, let's have a look at this nappy you like wearing then. Is it a disposable one?", Margaret said laughing.

I pulled my pyjama bottoms down a bit and in a loud voice shouted, "Ta-da!"

"Ah, a terry nappy. Ben, you make me laugh!"

We both laughed, and within a few seconds, the embarrassment, guilt, shame had all but disappeared.

"Well Ben, you're the first person to wear a nappy in my house," Margaret said.

"I'll be the last too, won't I?" I replied.

At Margaret's house, showing her what I had on.

For the next hour while playing cards and chatting, I just had my pyjama top on and a nappy and for the first time, I felt comfortable and not ashamed of who I was. It felt like I was in heaven, and I was having the best night of fun I'd had for what seemed ages.

It got to about 11.30 and Margaret said, "Right Ben, I think we better get off to bed, love. We will have to get up a bit earlier in the morning to set off, I think."

"Yeah okay, thanks for a great night," I replied.

"Ah your welcome lovey, I've had fun too. It's been nice having company all night and laughing with someone," she replied.

We cleaned up the front room a bit and then while we sat finishing our drinks, Margaret said "Ben, I'm not an expert, but you've had that on all night. Do you need to put a dry one on, love?"

"Yeah, but I haven't got a spare one with me. I only have this one," I replied.

"Hang on a minute, love," Margaret said, and went into the hall and brought back a clean towel. It wasn't a white one, more of an off white or very light grey colour, but it was the right size. She came back into the lounge and said, "Here you go, love, will this do?"

"Yeah thanks, Margaret," I replied.

"I'll put that on a wash tonight for you, otherwise it might smell in your room and you can use this tomorrow if you still want to wear one," Margaret said.

End of the night and being advised to change my nappy.

I went upstairs and took off my now soaked nappy, had a quick wash and put on the towel Margaret had given me, followed by the plastic pants. It felt so much better in a dry nappy. I hadn't realised how much I had used the other one until I took it off. As I got my top back on, Margaret came in.

"Wow, you're changed already love, that was quick! Right, I'll take this nappy and put it in the washer, Ben. Sleep well, night, night love."

"Okay night night, Margaret and thank you."

She left the room, turning the light off as she went and I climbed into bed and for a while just lay there thinking about what a good night we had and how relieved I was at being able to talk to someone about why I wore nappies and so on. I quickly drifted off to sleep and before long, Margaret was waking me up for breakfast.

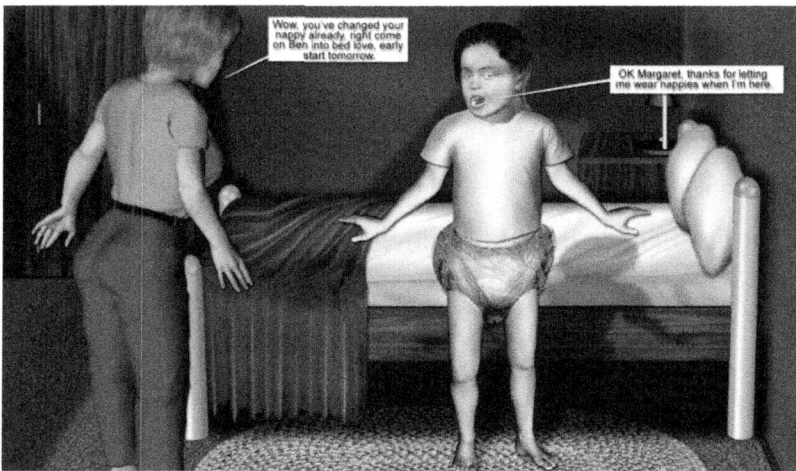

Fresh nappy on for bed. I was getting good at it.

"Morning, Ben," Margaret said.

"Morning," I replied groggily.

I got out of bed and quickly remembered that I still had a nappy on.

"Wow," I thought. "This feels great!" and with a quick check realised that I hadn't used it during the night.

I put my pyjama bottoms on and went downstairs into the kitchen where Margaret was making a cup of tea for us both. I now realised that this nappy felt a bit bulky and was a bit noticeable under my pyjama bottoms. I wasn't bothered though, remembering what had happened the night before and just sat down at the table. That was a weird feeling too and one I remembered from my childhood, sitting on a hard chair and feeling comfy as my nappy was again acting as a cushion.

"Here you go, Ben," said Margaret, handing me a brew.

"Thanks, Margaret," I replied and took a welcome sip of the tea she had made.

"Did you sleep okay, love?" she asked.

"Yeah. Really well thank you. I could have slept all day!" I replied, laughing a little.

We chatted a little about the previous night and the trip we were going on soon.

"Right Ben, go and get a shower and get yourself dressed darling. Leave that nappy on the landing and I'll sort it out, okay?"

I went upstairs and took off the dry nappy, leaving it on the landing as instructed and after heading to the loo, jumped into the shower. I grabbed a towel and wrapped it around myself and headed to the bedroom to get dressed for the day. As it was summer, I had brought shorts, a t-shirt and a pair of trainers for the trip as well as long pants just in case. As I entered the bedroom, I immediately noticed on the bed, the wet nappy I had taken off last night, clean and folded on the bed with the pins and plastic pants on top. I remembered now that I had asked Margaret if I could wear my nappy that day. I took this as a sign it was still okay and after drying myself, laid on the floor, took my time and put my nappy on. I stood up and adjusted everything so that it felt comfortable and then put my shorts and t-shirt on. I then sat on the bed and put my socks and trainers on.

It felt so strange doing this. I could tell I was wearing a nappy as when I lifted my foot, it was a little more difficult than normal crossing my leg to tie my laces. My nappy made it a little more difficult to move each leg. I was soon ready and headed downstairs where Margaret was in the front room with a fresh cup of tea for us both. I picked up my brew sat down on the chair and asked Margaret if I could have a ciggie.

"Of course, love. Here you go," she replied.

She handed me a ciggie and lit the lighter for me. I then sat down and enjoyed the fresh tea whilst having a puff on the cigarette - something I had never done before.

"Thanks for washing that towel for me," I said.

"That's okay, Ben," she replied laughing, "I've never washed a nappy before."

Margaret was being so kind and understanding and it was such a nice feeling to be able to do this and not feel ashamed of what I was wearing.

"Have you put your nappy back on for today?" Margaret enquired.

"Yeah, I put the white one back on. It's okay still to wear it today?" I asked.

"Of course, Ben. Don't worry, your secret is safe with me," Margaret replied. "You can wear what you want, Ben. It doesn't matter to me at all. You're not hurting anyone are you?"

"No, but it's not normal for someone my age to want to wear a nappy is it?" I replied.

"Well no, it was a bit of a shock when you told me last night after I saw it, but that was only because it was unexpected. I've seen plenty in my time, Ben, I can assure you, but I've never known anyone wanting to wear nappies. That is a first I must admit, but it most certainly is not wrong, and you must never be ashamed of being you, do you understand, love?"

"I think so Margaret, I've never been able to talk to anyone about it until now, only Scot and his mum years ago," I explained.

"Well, you can talk to me about anything, but you must remember that not everyone will be as accepting or understand like I am, or Scot was. Some will see you as different and although you are normal, will make out that you are not."

"Yeah, I know, but thanks for being kind."

Margaret's words stuck with me for years after this. She was so right in that. Of course, I was normal. There was nothing wrong with what I was doing, but other people would never see it that way and would make fun or criticise it, if they knew what I was wearing. That was a chance I would never take and as I got older, I soon realised that being different made you a target for hate and bullying, and I suppose I felt lucky in that I could hide my difference and keep my unusual behaviour as a secret only I knew about. Even if I decided to wear one again, being able to wear clothes over the top, hid the fact what I was actually wearing.

We were soon on our way to St Anne's, it was a lovely sunny day and I was really happy and looking forward to our day trip. The start of the trip kind of took me back to when I was six and heading for Blackpool, looking at all the new buildings that had appeared since I last took this route. I had decided that I wouldn't use the nappy I was wearing as, I soon realised I hadn't brought a spare. This was fine by me though. Just the fact of wearing it was wonderful.

A Ford Cortina like Margaret's. What a cool car it was.

Margaret was soon singing along with the songs playing on the radio and I was laughing at her, making jokes about her voice.

"You cheeky bugger," Margaret said.

"Don't give up your day job!" I replied, cheekily.

Margaret then said, "Why are you being shy anyway Ben? I know you've got a nappy on, don't I and you said you liked just wearing it with no trousers on last night. Remember?"

She was right. I did take my pyjama bottoms off last night and enjoyed it too. I didn't feel embarrassed the previous night, so I thought may as well do the same again and I slipped my shorts off, threw them on the back seat and then sat back down. It felt so good and free doing this. I didn't care at all at how I must have looked. This was me - the me that liked doing this and I trusted Margaret. We were both laughing and having such a good time that nothing could have spoiled this at all.

Yeah, I was just wearing a nappy in the car, but I didn't care. Why should I? To me at that time it was fun, Margaret didn't mind and in fact, she encouraged me to do it.

En route to St Anne's. This was a great trip.

Most people would probably think this was wrong of her, but I don't. I trusted her completely as if she was my mum, and if she was going to do anything that was considered improper, she had been given every opportunity last night and all the times I had been in her house before on my own. She was just a kind, caring and open-minded individual who was the first person who had allowed me to express myself in a safe environment without any feeling of guilt or shame - something which I will always be grateful for. The previous night and that day, I had been allowed to let all my thoughts and emotions out, while feeling protected by an adult to whom I could talk openly and maybe get some answers about what I was doing.

The journey continued uneventfully and once we were about ten minutes away, Margaret said I should probably cover my nappy up to be safe. As we drove to Brenda's, I could now see what Margaret meant about the place. It was a really nice area and totally different from Blackpool. Margaret pointed out different things to me and I asked her about the place as well. Eventually, we arrived at Brenda's where we were warmly greeted and made to feel at home. Brenda gave me a drink of pop and a bag of crisps and said I could play in the garden if I wanted while she had a chat with Margaret. The garden was huge and I found a football and started kicking it about and enjoying the sun. I felt really at ease and comfortable, even though I had a nappy on. I didn't care at all, but I ensured that it was kept hidden. As Margaret had said, and I had understood, not all people would see this as innocently as Margaret or me.

I must have been playing for about an hour when I needed the loo. I went in and Brenda told me where the toilet was. As I locked the door I double-checked to make sure it wouldn't open, as I had to unpin one side of my nappy, so I could have a wee. I washed my hands and then pinned my nappy back on and pulled up my plastic pants and shorts and headed back downstairs. This felt really great and natural to me, and I was getting used to having a nappy on too and forgetting about it. Margaret gave me a little wink and nod as I went back into the front room and I smiled back. We stayed at Brenda's for about three hours or so before Margaret asked me if I wanted an ice cream and a drink from somewhere. I didn't need asking twice for an ice cream and we were soon walking down the promenade towards the cafes and shops.

"You okay, Ben?" Margaret asked.

"Yeah I'm having a nice time," I replied.

"Have you kept your nappy dry, love?" she asked.

"I have, yeah. I used the toilet before, as I didn't want to wee in it."

"That's fine, love, as long as you're okay."

Margaret bought us an ice cream each and we sat on the sea wall enjoying the weather and watching people on the beach. I remember thinking at the time, I would have given anything at that moment to have taken my shorts off and ran and played about on the beach, but I knew this couldn't be, even if Margaret had said I could. I wouldn't have had the courage to do it for fear of humiliation and stares from other people. They wouldn't know how I was feeling about what I was doing and that to me, wearing a nappy was normal.

They would see me as weird or something worse maybe. It was soon time to head back to the car and start the journey home. Margaret had promised my mum I would be home for tea. As we got in the car, it was roasting hot as it had been in the sun all day. No sooner had I got in I removed my shorts and looked over to Margaret and smiled.

"Is that better now, lovey?" Margaret asked with a smile.

"It is. I'm not embarrassed in front of you, Margaret," I replied.

"Good, you don't need to be either."

We set off on our journey and I think the hot weather, early morning and so on had taken its toll, as I soon drifted off to sleep. Margaret woke me about ten minutes from her house as I would have to get dressed again.

"Hello, sleepyhead. You've been out cold!" Margaret said.

"Have I? I was tired."

"Have you had a nice time?" she asked.

"Brilliant, I've loved it, last night and today were fab," I replied honestly.

"That's good then, I hope you will come and see me when I move Ben, now that you know how nice it is," Margaret said.

"I will come and see you if my mum will let me, I promise," I replied.

We were soon at Margaret's and after dumping our bags in the hallway, I put the kettle on to make a brew. Margaret came in with a lit ciggie for me, as I would have to go home soon and we both sat at the table drinking our brew and puffing away on our ciggies.

"Are you taking your nappy off before you go home love?" Margaret asked.

"Yeah, can I leave it here please, as I can't hide it anywhere at home and if my mum finds it I will be in trouble?" I replied.

"Course you can darling. When you take it off, leave it on the bed and I'll sort it out for you."

"Thank you for letting me wear a nappy, Margaret. I've loved it," I exclaimed.

As instructed, once I had removed my nappy and put my underpants back on, I left the nappy, pins and pants on the bed and went back downstairs. It felt weird having normal underwear back on again. I was sad that I wouldn't be able to wear it for a while, but was so glad I had some great memories from last night and today to remind me of it. I said goodbye to Margaret and told her I would be back in a couple of days for any errands or jobs and gave her a hug.

As I headed back home, I couldn't help but smile both on the inside and outside. This was my first experience of wearing a nappy freely and not being made to feel guilty, shy or embarrassed in any way whatsoever. To this day, I still think about the things Margaret said to me and the advice she gave and it has served me well. Little did she know the experience I'd had both the previous night and that day would be the only one of its kind until I was much older.

Margaret moved away about two months later and I did get to wear my nappy again on two more occasions, not openly, but under my clothes and as she had promised, she took my nappy set with her when she moved to look after for me stating that she would keep them safe for when I visit, something that I didn't do until I was 21.

Life continued as normal for me once Margaret left. I didn't get the chance to wear a proper nappy again and if I'm being honest I never really thought much about it. I did still look back with fondness on the times I spent with Margaret and my whole nappy wearing experience and I still smile about it to this day.

Epilogue:

At sixteen, having left school with very poor qualifications, I opted to join the Army and for the next seven years, this was my life. I could write a whole chapter and more about my time in the forces and maybe one day I will, but in summary, the army made me into the man I am today. I served in three conflicts and was awarded medals and citations for my exemplary service. There's another thing to consider. Here I was in the army, fighting for Queen and Country, a rufty tufty soldier and I liked to wear nappies! Can you fathom that one out? But is there anything to fathom out when all said and done?

Looking back through this book, it's clear to me that I must have been programmed - or maybe destined - to like wearing nappies. There is absolutely nothing I can do about it - trust me, I have tried. I have been through every emotion there is about why I do it and I've never really found an answer. With the passage of time, the internet and social media have shown me that there are thousands of people all over the world like me that wear a nappy, both female and male and every age for that matter too. Some of these people wear a nappy constantly, as I would assume the desire is too overpowering for them to control. You have to ask yourself though, is there an answer? I don't think there is, certainly not one that fits every person that does like to put a nappy on.

We are who we are - and does it matter what either you or I do to make us happy? Let me put it another way. On a Friday night after getting home from work, I take a shower, have some tea and then when I'm ready will put a nappy on (these days a disposable one), grab a beer and watch a film.

Another person will snort a line of cocaine, another dress up in ladies clothing, another decides to get naked and walk around his or her garden. The point I'm trying to make is that we are all different and that's what makes us unique individuals, so I can't understand why people choose to ridicule or mock someone when they are just different to themselves. I am sure we all have a particular "thing" that we like. Mine just happens to be nappies and has been since I was six, and I can't escape it, although I can control it now.

Wearing a nappy allows me to release my stress and worries and be happy. That's all it is - nothing more, nothing less, and I'm not harming anyone. The AB/DL community are still, and probably will always be frowned upon. I am neither an AB or DL. I am *me*. I do what I do, as it's what I want, need or have to do. I don't like labels and I will never give myself one. I am like you, a normal human being with my own desires, thoughts and guilty pleasures.

So, whatever yours is, enjoy it. No one has the right to judge you. Those that do are either jealous or do not understand. If they don't understand and only mock what they don't understand, then, in my opinion, they are ignorant. A true friend, partner, husband, wife or family member should accept you for who you are or what you do, if you decide to be open and honest with them. If they don't that, is their problem and not yours.

I've been a soldier and fought three times for my country. Would it have mattered if I'd done this wearing a nappy under my combats to make me feel happy? I also hold down a professional job and have done so for years. I have a loving partner and occasionally, I go out and get drunk. Most days, I go about my daily life and yet I wear a nappy. Why should I be treated any differently or mocked? My partner accepts me for who I am, not for what I do. She understands and accepts me for the heart I have, the love I can give and the unquestionable support, both emotionally and physically I can give her without question and the family that we have become.

One of my beliefs in life is *'treat everyone with the same respect as to how you would like to be treated'*. I don't care who or what you are, you are a person with the same right to enjoy your life whatever that entails and if you are not hurting, annoying or disrespecting anyone else, then why does it really matter? You are here on this earth for one lifetime - that's it. No second chances, no re-runs and so I ask you this - why must people judge others when that other person does something that is outside their understanding or beliefs?

Society tells us we should act normally, but the answer to the big question that most will be searching for from now until they die is *"what is normal"*.

Well here is the answer...

You are normal, and I am normal. I'm just not exactly like you, and that's alright.

To be continued.........

Now that you have read this book you might be interested in more of our books. Go to https://abdiscovery.com.au/ **to find our complete collection of AB fiction and non-fiction.**

I am unique.
I am special.
I am me.

I AM WHO I AM.
I LIKE WHAT I LIKE.
I LOVE WHAT I LOVE.
I DO WHAT I WANT.
GET OFF MY BACK
AND DEAL WITH IT,
IT'S MY LIFE,
NOT YOURS.

Printed in Great Britain
by Amazon

29222647R00111